Appliquilt™

for
Christmas

Tonee White

That Patchwork Place®

Dedication

To my parents, Hank and Irene Spiekerman, for making my early Christmases magical and for instilling the importance of tradition in me and in their grand-children. I love you both.

Acknowledgments

Thanks go to:

My family for their help in all my endeavors;

The Coven, my quilting group, for their encouragement, patience, and support; and

Margrit for her technical advice and for bringing me back down to earth at times.

Credits

Editor-in-Chief .... Barbara Weiland
Technical Editor .... Melissa Lowe
Managing Editor .... Greg Sharp
Copy Editor .... Tina Cook
Proofreader .... Leslie Phillips
Design Director ....Judy Petry
Text and Cover Designer .... Cheryl Stevenson
Design Assistant .... Claudia L'Heureux
Photographer .... Brent Kane
Technical Illustrator .... Lisa McKenney
Decorative Art .... Barb Tourtillotte

Appliquilt™ for Christmas
© 1995 by Tonee White
That Patchwork Place, Inc., PO Box 118, Bothell, WA 98041-0118 USA

Printed in the United States of America
00 99 98 97 96 95   6 5 4 3 2 1

Library of Congress Cataloging-in-Publication Data

White, Tonee,
    Appliquilt for Christmas / Tonee White.
        p.   cm.
    ISBN 1-56477-106-7 (pbk.)
    1. Appliqué—Patterns. 2. Quilts. 3. Christmas decorations.
    I. Title.
    TT779.W552   1995
    746.46—dc20   95-893
                                                        CIP

Mission Statement

We are dedicated to providing quality products that encourage creativity and promote self-esteem in our customers and our employees.

We strive to make a difference in the lives we touch.

That Patchwork Place is an employee-owned, financially secure company.

Contents

Meet the Author

Tonee White lives in Irvine, California, where she spends her time teaching quilting, writing quilt books, and creating quilts. She recently retired from her career as a registered nurse to devote herself to quilting full time.

This is Tonee's second book featuring her wonderful Appliquilt™ technique, which combines appliqué and quilting in one easy step.

This book was inspired by Tonee's love of the Christmas season. She says "the celebration of Christmas has always been very special in my life, so a book full of designs related to this holiday was a natural." The quilts featured here are some of Tonee's favorites.

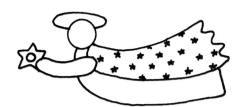

Introduction

'Tis the season to be jolly and rushed and busy and harried. Christmas must be the most popular holiday; I know it is at our house. It's in my thoughts, from time to time, throughout the year. The planning, shopping, wrapping, and cooking are all part of this wonderful time.

The traditions we continue and the new ones we create for our children and grandchildren are the cement that bonds families together and makes them strong. Christmas "work" is time well spent. The house is shining, the gifts are wrapped, a Christmas carol can be heard, and "something good" smells are in the air. Although we moan and groan and complain about it, we wouldn't have it any other way. The preparation and anticipation is the best part, and the greatest rewards are reaped when you know you've pleased "them."

Because of our busy schedules, we have precious little time to complete all the tasks we've planned to make this "the best Christmas ever." This year, Appliquilt comes to the rescue.

This method is not only fun, but at Christmas it is a blessing. You can pick it up for ten minutes at a time or spend a day and do a whole project. It's portable. In the few minutes it takes to get to church on Sunday, you can get a few of your appliqué pieces sewn on. During the holidays the most precious commodity is neither frankincense nor myrrh—it's time.

I am certain that there is a wealth of untapped creativity in all of you. The fact that you purchased this book is proof. I offer these designs as suggestions and inspirations; use your creativity and make them your own.

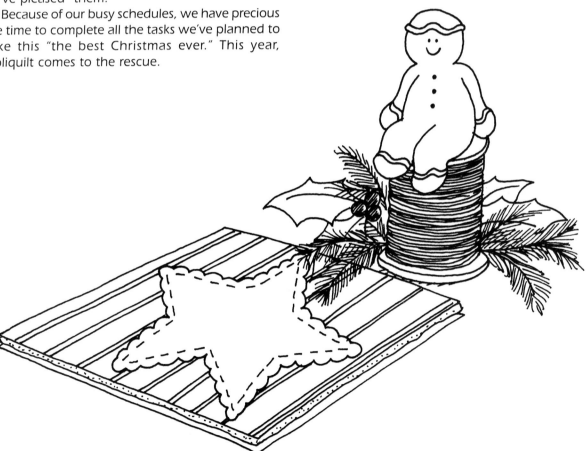

Choosing Fabric and Supplies

Fabric

When it comes to choosing fabric, a chorus of moans can usually be heard. Come on, this is the first fun part of your project! You can either go shopping for new fabric or you can use some of your fabric "stash" and go shopping for new fabric later. There are lots of opportunities to be creative.

While selecting fabrics for your appliquilt projects, keep in mind that you will sew through at least four layers: the appliqué piece, quilt top, batting, and backing. Anything that you can put a needle through will work, but remember that some fabrics are easier to needle than others. The term "needle" refers to the way that your needle moves through the fabric as you stitch.

We want this to be fun and easy. Soft cotton, homespun, and woven fabrics are a pleasure to work with and look wonderful in these designs. Stiffer fabrics, such as batiks, are more difficult to work with. By all means, use any fabric that makes your quilt as wonderful as it can be.

Setting Dye

Although I do not always prewash my fabrics, I do test most of them for colorfastness (particularly red and teal fabrics). Take a small piece of the colored fabric and a small piece of a white fabric and rub them together under running tap water. If dye from the colored fabric bleeds onto the white fabric, I use the recipe below to set the dye. If the dye bleeds onto the white fabric after I've treated the fabric twice, I return it to the store. I want to complain to someone, as well as give the shopkeeper the opportunity to warn others who purchase the fabric.

Recipe for Setting Fabric Dye
2 cups white vinegar per washer load

Prewash the fabric and add the white vinegar to the second rinse cycle of your washer. Repeat the colorfastness test described above. If the dye still bleeds onto the white fabric, repeat the washing and vinegar and test again.

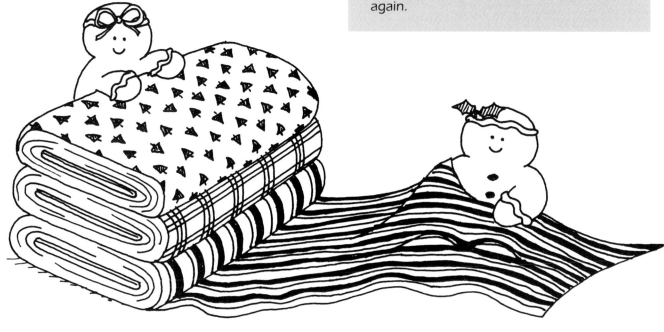

Tea Dyeing

I use tea-dyed fabric a lot. Some fabrics dye better than others. Loosely woven and muslin fabrics really soak up the dye, while more tightly woven fabrics or those with a smoother finish may not soak up the dye at all.

Prewash fabric before tea dyeing to remove the manufacturer's finish and sizing treatments. Fabric that has been treated with finish or sizing is more likely to resist tea dyeing. You may have to wash the fabric repeatedly.

I sometimes add a cup of bleach to the washer load when I'm prewashing my fabric to begin the aging process. The bleach seems to enhance the ability of the fabric to soak up the tea dye.

Nancy Kirk of the Kirk Collection in Omaha, Nebraska, washes fabric in the dishwasher. The abrasiveness and the bleach in dishwasher detergent gives fabric an aged look.

Recipe for Tea Dyeing
1 quart hot tap water
3 tablespoons instant coffee
8 tea bags

Stir instant coffee into water. Let the tea bags steep in the mixture for a few minutes; remove tea bags and soak prewashed fabric in the tea dye for twenty minutes. Soak longer or even overnight to get darker results. To get a blotchy effect, leave the tea bags in the water with the fabric.

If your tea-dyed fabric is not splotchy enough, try soaking cotton balls or small pieces of wadded muslin in a cup with hot water, two tea bags, and a little of the coffee left over from your morning brew. Place the cotton balls or pieces of muslin on dry fabric and let sit for thirty minutes to one hour. Rinse and dry the fabric.

You can also deepen or add color after you have finished the project. Hang the quilt outside on a clothesline. Prepare the tea dye as described above and pour it into a spray bottle. Spray your quilt all over or in selected spots and let air dry. Since the fabric is not as saturated using this method, rinsing is not necessary.

Grunging Fabric

To tea-dye is wonderful, to "grunge" is divine. Grunging is a technique I developed to permanently wrinkle fabric, giving it an old, worn look. The angel's wings in "'Tis the Season" on page 19 and the quote background in "O Christmas Tree" on page 22 are made from grunged fabric.

To grunge fabric, you need the stiffest muslin you can find. The stiffer the fabric, the grungier you can make it.

Wet the fabric thoroughly. Squeeze it into a ball, wringing out excess water. When you have removed as much water as possible, put the fabric ball in the dryer. Dry the fabric on the hottest setting. If the fabric is stiff enough, it will remain in a ball throughout the drying process. I usually grunge ½-yard or smaller pieces of fabric. Larger pieces are less likely to hold together while drying.

When the fabric is completely dry (be sure to check the center of the ball), smooth it flat. You may have to use an iron to smooth your fabric flat enough to cut out appliqué pieces. If the fabric was stiff enough to hold together in the dryer, you won't be able to iron out the wrinkles.

You can tea-dye this fabric or use it as is; grunged fabric adds texture and interest to your quilts.

Supplies

Embellishments

Buttons, ribbons, trinkets, and other decorations are fun to collect and fun to use, and they spark creativity. There isn't a better way to add texture, dimension, and interest to a quilt.

I am always on the lookout for embellishments and am delighted when I find things to add to my stash. Christmas-oriented embellishments are available year 'round in many craft and fabric shops. Use your imagination while shopping as well as while creating your quilt. You can attach almost anything and anything goes.

The "Resource List" on page 16 contains sources for many of the embellishments used in this book. See "Adding Embellishments" on pages 14–15 for information on attaching decorations to your quilt.

Batting

You will stitch through at least four layers, so you need a lightweight batting that is easy to needle. I use Pellon™ fleece almost exclusively in my appliquilt projects. It is thin and less dense than similar battings.

If you hold a piece of Pellon fleece up to the light you can see through it. This will help you recognize it when shopping. I think the Pellon fleece works best, but Warm & Natural™ batting is a good choice if Pellon fleece is not available.

Thread

There are so many stitching mediums on the market today! I try each new one, but my favorite is #8 perle cotton. I use this more than any other. The tightly twisted strands do not separate. It is thick enough to give a primitive look, yet thin enough to glide through the quilt "sandwich" easily. If you visit a needlework shop, you will find #8 perle cotton in many colors and shades.

I use embroidery floss (three or four strands), linen, or metallic thread when I need a finer thread or want to add a glitzy touch. You can separate the strands of embroidery floss for delicate designs. Heavy-duty quilting thread does not show as well as embroidery floss or perle cotton.

For most of the projects in this book, I used perle cotton or embroidery floss in a contrasting color. The contrast between the fabric and the stitches adds to the primitive look, creates visual interest, and helps define the appliqué pieces. For a more refined look, try a quilting thread in the same color as the appliqué piece.

If you run across new stitching mediums, give them a try. You might find some you really like. Just remember, you want strength and ease of needling.

Scissors and Rotary-Cutting Blades

When I teach classes, one of the most frequently asked questions is "What kind of scissors do you use?" My favorite pair of scissors is a wave-blade pinking shear made by Clover®. These weigh less than most pinking shears and take less of a "bite" out of your fabric than other pinking shears.

It is important to pink your appliqué pieces to reduce fraying and give the edges interest. There are a variety of pinking and scalloping shears as well as pinking and wave rotary-cutting blades available. When you go shopping for pinking shears, take a scrap of fabric and try the shears before buying them. Make sure that the shears are sharp and don't "chew up" the fabric as you cut.

I do recommend the pinking and wave blades, but be aware of the differences between these blades and the conventional straight blade.

I have found that I can cut through only two layers of fabric at one time with a rotary cutter. When I use a pinking or wave blade, I apply more pressure than usual to the rotary cutter because it is difficult to recut the fabric if the blade has not cleanly cut the entire line. Align the blade with the cut fabric edges to avoid chewing up the edge.

There are a number of scissors on the market with shaped blades designed for use with paper. These do not cut fabric!

Needles

I prefer to appliquilt with embroidery needles. I usually purchase a variety package containing sizes Number 3 though 9. Number 3 needles are larger than necessary for perle cotton, but I occasionally use them for heavier thread. You can use Number 8 and Number 9 needles for embroidery floss or lighter-weight threads.

I choose the smallest possible needle that will accommodate my thread. Smaller needles create less drag when you pull them through the layers of the quilt, and they are easier to control.

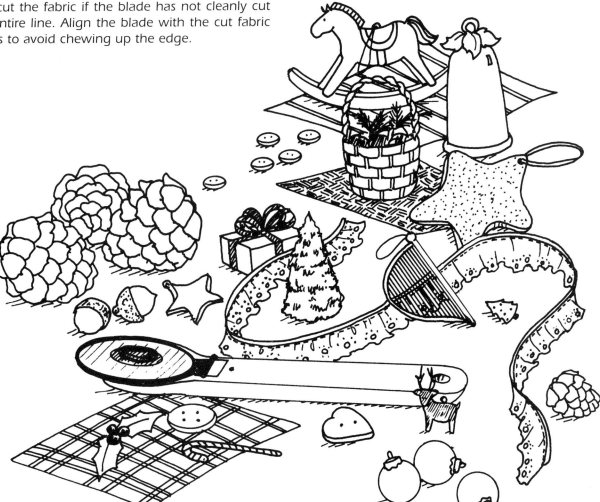

Quilting and appliquéing in one step requires that you make a "quilt sandwich" or foundation first. To do this, the three layers of the quilt—top, batting, and backing—must be sewn or pinned together.

In many of the projects in this book, you stitch the background blocks and borders onto the batting and backing fabric rather than piecing the entire quilt top first. This "sew-and-flip" technique allows you to quilt your project as you piece the top. I do not tape or clamp the backing fabric in these situations.

Cut the backing fabric at least 2" larger than the top on all sides. This allows your top to "creep" out a bit as you stitch. I've included at least 2" allowances for the projects in this book. With the wrong side of the backing fabric facing up, tape it to a hard, flat surface, such as a floor or tabletop. Using masking tape or clamps, secure the fabric so that it is smooth and fairly taut. Cut the batting the same size as your backing fabric. Lay the batting on top of the backing and smooth it, working from the center out to the edges.

Add the background fabric or pieced top, smoothing it from the center outward. Pin-baste your quilt sandwich (I prefer medium-size safety pins). Place the pins approximately every 4". Smooth the fabric each time you place a pin. Do not close the pins until all are in place. If you close each pin as you go, the

backing may shift slightly, and by the time you have closed your last pin, the backing will have shifted quite a bit. After all the pins have been placed, close the pins and remove the tape.

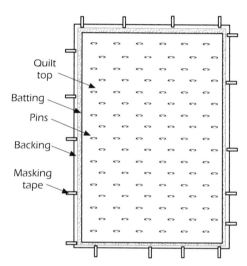

You can also hand baste your quilt sandwich. Starting from the center, stitch rows every 4" to 6" out to the edges of the quilt. Smooth the fabric as you stitch.

For some of these projects, I recommend hand or machine quilting "in-the-ditch" to help keep the sandwich from shifting while you appliqué. If you choose to quilt by hand, use either perle cotton or quilting thread and a running stitch, as shown on page 12. I machine quilt in-the-ditch using invisible nylon thread in my needle and cotton thread in my bobbin.

You can, at this point, trim your quilt sandwich and attach the binding. This makes a neat portable project.

Cutting Out the Appliqué Pieces

You need to make templates for all the projects in this book. I recommend using the heavy-weight, transparent template plastic that is sold in flat sheets. This is one of those things that makes our quilting lives easier. The template plastic that is sold in rolls wants to stay that way; it's a continuous fight to keep it flat while you trace and cut.

Trace your pattern shapes onto the template plastic. I use a #2 lead pencil for this. Using your paper scissors, cut the templates out on the traced line. Do not use your fabric scissors. Cutting plastic and paper with your fabric scissors dulls the blades.

To make the design exactly as it is pictured on the page, place the templates right side down on the wrong side of the fabric. I use a #2 lead pencil to trace designs on light- and medium-colored fabrics and a white or pastel chalk-type pencil to trace designs on dark fabrics. To make a reverse image of the design, place the templates right side up on the wrong side of the fabric. In many of these designs it does not matter if the image is reversed, but it is important if you are tracing letters such as R, S, or N.

Using your pinking shears, cut out the appliqué pieces on the traced line. Some pinking shears take quite a "bite" out of the fabric. I try to cut so that the traced line is in the middle of this bite. The appliqué pieces do not have to be cut precisely! Do not add seam allowances to the pieces; the templates are the finished size.

Appliquilting—
Appliqué & Quilting in One Step

I usually pin all the pieces on small- to medium-size quilts before stitching. On larger quilts, I complete one block at a time. If you pin too many pieces in place, you may displace some while stitching others.

Pin the appliqué pieces in place, overlapping them if necessary. I pin overlapping pieces out of the way when stitching, rather than removing them. This way, I do not disturb the original arrangement.

Make the stitches as long or short as you wish. Longer or uneven stitches add to the primitive look. I usually stitch about ¼" from the pinked edge. I stitch even closer to the edge if the appliqué piece is very small.

Start stitching on the top side of your project, leaving a 6"-long tail. Using a simple running or basting stitch, sew through all three layers.

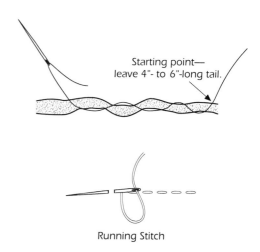

Starting point—
leave 4"- to 6"-long tail.

Running Stitch

Stitch back to where you began. End your stitching on the top side and tie the two tails together in a square knot (right over left, then left over right). Clip the tails to whatever length you like. I usually leave a ¼"-long tail.

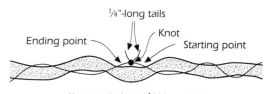

¼"-long tails

Ending point   Knot   Starting point

Knot and trim to ¼"-long tails.

If you run out of thread while stitching in a continuous line or around a large appliqué piece, end your stitching on top and leave a 6"-long tail. Start stitching where you ended, leaving another 6"-long tail. After you have taken a few stitches, tie the two tails together in a square knot and trim.

If you can't tie the two tails together, knot your thread before you begin and start on the top of your project. When you come to the end of your stitching, gently gather your last few stitches and make a knot on top of the quilt. Smooth out the gathers and the knot will lie snugly.

Binding the Edges

Appliquilt bindings are fun, fast, easy, and do not use much fabric.

Cut 1¼"- to 1½"-wide binding strips, using pinking shears or the pinking blade on your rotary cutter. Fold the strips in half lengthwise and, with wrong sides together, press. After you have trimmed the batting and backing to match the quilt top, wrap the binding strip around the edge of the quilt. Match the crease edge with the edge of your quilt and pin at the beginning and 6" to 8" from the first pin.

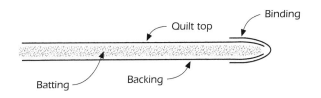

Binding

Quilt top

Batting

Backing

When you need to add another binding strip, simply overlap the ends of the binding strips 1". I usually take two stitches where the binding strips overlap. This method eliminates the need to sew binding strips together before you begin.

I arrange and pin the binding 10" to 12" ahead of my stitching. I do not pin all the way around the quilt. This eliminates pins that may scratch or prick me while I'm stitching.

Start stitching approximately 1" from the end of the binding strip. Using perle cotton, stitch about ¼" from the inside edge of the binding. Stitch through all the layers. Use the same running stitch you use for appliquilting.

Miter the corners as you approach them by folding and pinning. I take two stitches in the corners to secure the folds. Check the back of your quilt to make sure you catch the fold of the miters on the back as well as the front.

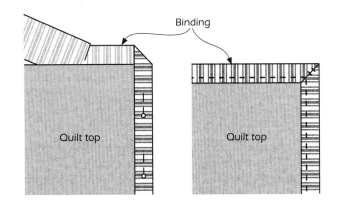

Binding

Binding

Quilt top

Quilt top

This binding method works well with appliquilt designs. However, if you have a favorite method that you would like to use, I'm sure it would look fine on your appliquilt.

Adding Embellishments

Embellishments put a finishing touch to these quilts and make them special by adding interest, texture, color, and charm.

I use different methods to attach different kinds of embellishments. When sewing buttons onto my projects, I use #8 perle cotton or several strands of embroidery floss. Start from the top side of the quilt, leaving a 4"- to 6"-long tail. Stitch through the holes in the buttons twice and tie a double knot on top to secure. Clip the tails to the desired length. I use the same method for adding beads, charms, lace, and most other embellishments.

To attach something that does not have holes, cut a 12" length of perle cotton. Using epoxy glue, attach the midpoint of the perle cotton to the back of the object. Make sure that your perle cotton is totally surrounded with glue. When the glue is dry, thread one end of the perle cotton through your needle and pull it through to the back of the quilt. Repeat with the other end. Tie a square knot; I usually knot this a third time. Depending on the size and weight of the object, you may need to use more than one strand of perle cotton.

For heavy or large objects, take a stitch on the back of the quilt before you tie the ends. This should hold the object snugly in place.

Another embellishment option is to add a ribbon bow with buttons sewn to the end of the ribbon. Experiment with silk flowers, leaves, or anything else you have. This is an opportunity to be creative and to personalize your quilt. Let your imagination loose and have fun!

Embroidery stitches add another interesting touch to your quilts. I've used French knots and the backstitch in these quilts.

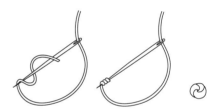

French Knot

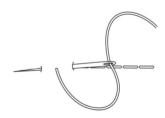

Backstitch

Yo-Yos

I use yo-yos as embellishments and to make designs such as the wreath in "'Tis the Season" and the Christmas tree in "Yo-Yo Christmas." To make yo-yos, trace the circle templates onto fabric and cut them out with pinking shears. Cut a length of perle cotton or a few strands of embroidery floss about 18" long and knot it about 6" from one end. Holding the fabric circle in one hand, right side facing you, stitch ¼" from the pinked edge. Use a running stitch around the entire edge of the circle, gathering the fabric against the knot as you stitch.

When you have stitched around the entire circle, flatten the yo-yo with the gathered edges in the center of one side and tie the two thread ends together. If you pull the gathers too tight, the yo-yo will not lie flat. Leave a small hole in the middle where the gathers come together. I leave a hole about the size of my index finger. Do not remove the thread from the needle.

Position the yo-yo on your quilt with the gathered side facing up. Take one stitch through the yo-yo and quilt, then string a button or bead on your thread and arrange it in the middle of the yo-yo. Take two more stitches to sew the button and yo-yo onto the quilt. End your stitching on top. Tie the threads in a square knot and trim.

If you use a shank button you will have to end your stitching and tie off on the back of the quilt.

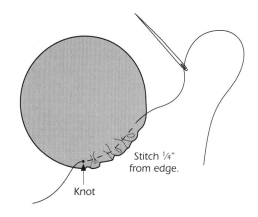

Stitch ¼" from edge.

Knot

Laundering Appliquilts

I've been asked if it is safe to launder these little quilts. If your knots have been tied securely, they can be laundered with care. Wash them by hand or in the machine on the gentle cycle. Air dry on a flat surface. Do not hang to dry, as they will stretch out of shape. The edges of the appliqué pieces may curl up a bit, but they can be pressed flat. You may like the "curly" look. It adds dimension to the quilt.

Resource List

You can purchase some of the more difficult-to-find materials, tools, and embellishments described in this book from the following suppliers.

Tools and Supplies

Clover
For store locations, call 1-800-233-1703
Wave-blade pinking shears

Embellishments

Michaels
For store locations, call 1-800-642-4235
Red beads, Santa's list, trumpet, and FIMO™ modeling compound

Country Loft
8166 La Mesa Boulevard
La Mesa, CA 91941
Tin heart and tea towel

Julian Country Store
P.O. Box 1000
Julian, CA 92036
Miniature rolling pin

Sugar Babies
1435 Salvadori Circle
Corona, CA 91720
Cinnamon buttons

The Wonderful, Whimsical Appliquilts

"Favorite Things" by Tonee White, 1993, Irvine, California, 38½" x 41½". Add your Christmas favorites to this wonderful sampler.

"Yo-Yo Christmas" by Tonee White, 1993, Irvine, California, 26" x 26". Make yo-yos the easy Appliquilt way!

"Yo-Yo Christmas" by Suzanne Dentt, 1994, El Cajon, California, 25½" x 24½".

"Tis the Season" by Tonee White, 1993, Irvine, California, 46" x 40". This quilt is chock full of all the things that come to mind when Christmas is mentioned.

"Tis the Season" by Janet Czernek, 1994, Huntington Beach, California, 46" x 40½".

"Christmas Dreams" by Tonee White, 1993, Irvine, California, 30½" x 39½". This quilt illustrates the magic Christmas holds for your favorite little ones.

"Christmas Goose" by
Tonee White, 1993,
Irvine, California,
26" x 22½". The goose
is the main attraction
at many a holiday
meal. Why not hang it
in the dining room?

"Christophe Dreams" by Aiko Kriz,
1994, Newport Beach, California,
29½" x 38½".

"Angel Sampler" by Tonee White, 1993, Irvine, California, 19½" x 30½". Peace is the hope we share at Christmas and all year 'round.

Every tree through-out the world bloomed and bore fruit on Christmas Eve

"O Christmas Tree" by Tonee White, 1993, Irvine, California, 17½" x 34". This quilt is a lovely way to recognize the true spirit of the Christmas season.

"Angels in the Stars" by Tonee White,
1993, Irvine, California, 24" x 28". A star
guides our angels through the night sky.

"Flying Angels" by Priscilla Stellrecht,
1994, Fullerton, California, 25" x 20".

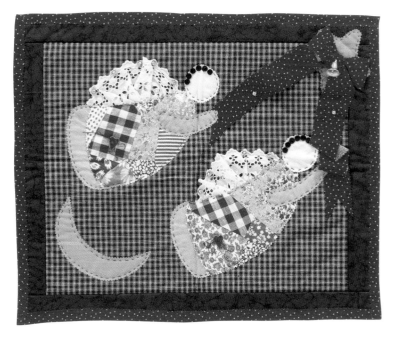

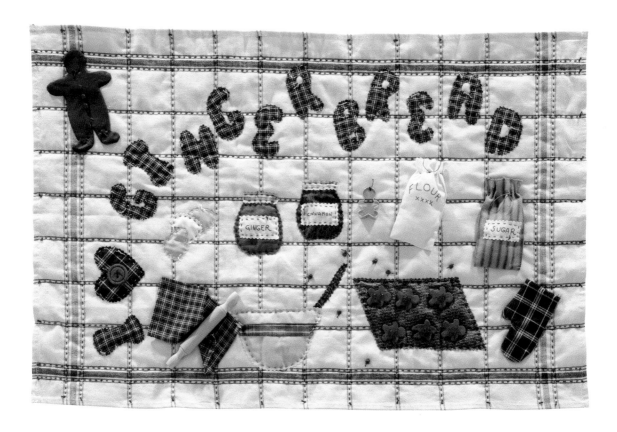

"I ❤ Gingerbread" by Tonee White, 1994, Irvine, California, 18" x 28". All you need to add to this quilt is your special recipe.

"Christmas Joy" by Tonee White, 1994, Irvine, California; each piece is approximately 11" x 17". Just one of these "letters" is a wonderful wall hanging; all three hung together proclaim the feeling of the season.

Angels in the Stars

You might want to tea-dye or bleach your fabric for this quilt. The angel design inspired one of my students, Priscilla Stellrecht, to use antique lace for the angels' wings and pieces of a treasured family quilt for their dresses.

Color Photo: page 23
Size: 24" x 28"
Materials: 44"-wide fabric

½ yd. (or fat quarter) small-scale plaid for background

⅓ yd. large-scale plaid for border

¼ yd. check for ribbon (or purchase 1 yd. of 1½"-wide ribbon) and binding

28" x 32" piece of fabric for backing

28" x 32" piece of Pellon fleece or other thin batting

⅛ to ¼ yd. each or scraps of the following:

Plaids and/or stripes for pinafores
Tea-dyed muslin for slip and sleeves
Muslin for faces
Print for moon and star

Lace doily for wings

#8 perle cotton in assorted colors

Embellishments of your choice, such as bells, beads, and heart-shaped buttons

Making the Foundation
Cutting

From the small-scale plaid fabric, cut:
   1 rectangle, 18" x 22", for background

From the large-scale plaid fabric, cut:
   2 strips, each 3½" x 18", for side borders
   2 strips, each 3½" x 28", for top and bottom
   borders

From the checked fabric, cut:
   3 strips, each 1½" x 44", for binding
   1 strip, 1½" x 36", for ribbon

Assembly

All seams are ¼" wide.

1. Layer the batting on the backing fabric. Smooth the batting and backing, working out from the center. See "Making the Quilt Sandwich Foundation" on page 10.
2. Place the 18" x 22" background on the center of the batting.
3. Align the 3½" x 18" plaid strips with the sides of the background, right sides together, and pin. Stitch through all the layers.

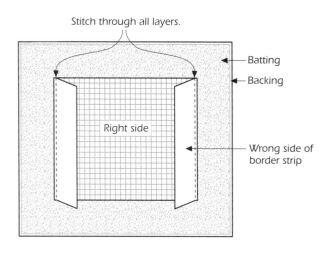

Stitch through all layers.

Batting

Backing

Right side

Wrong side of border strip

4. Flip the border strips right side up onto the batting. Press the seams.

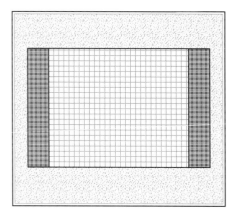

5. Sew the two 3½" x 28" plaid strips to the top and bottom of the background, right sides together, as you did with the side borders. Press the seams. Your completed foundation should look like the illustration below.

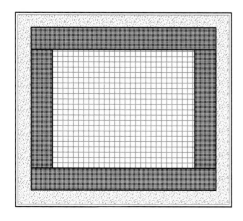

6. Bind the edges with the 1½" x 44"-wide checked strips, following the directions on page 13.

Appliquilt

Use the templates on page 27 and on the pull-out pattern. Refer to the templates and the quilt plan on page 25 for layout. The numbers on the templates indicate the stitching order.

1. Make plastic templates, following the directions on page 11.
2. Cut the appliqué pieces from the fabrics described in the "Materials" list. Cut the lace doily in half for the angels' wings.
3. Stitch the star in the upper right corner. Using the 1½" x 36" checked strip or length of ribbon, tie a bow and pin it to the star. Stitch in place.
4. Place the pinafore over the cut edge of the doily and stitch.
5. Stitch the moon and remaining angel pieces to the background. Stitch the ends of the bow underneath the angels' arms.

Embellishments

Stitch the bells, beads, and buttons in place, referring to the templates for placement.

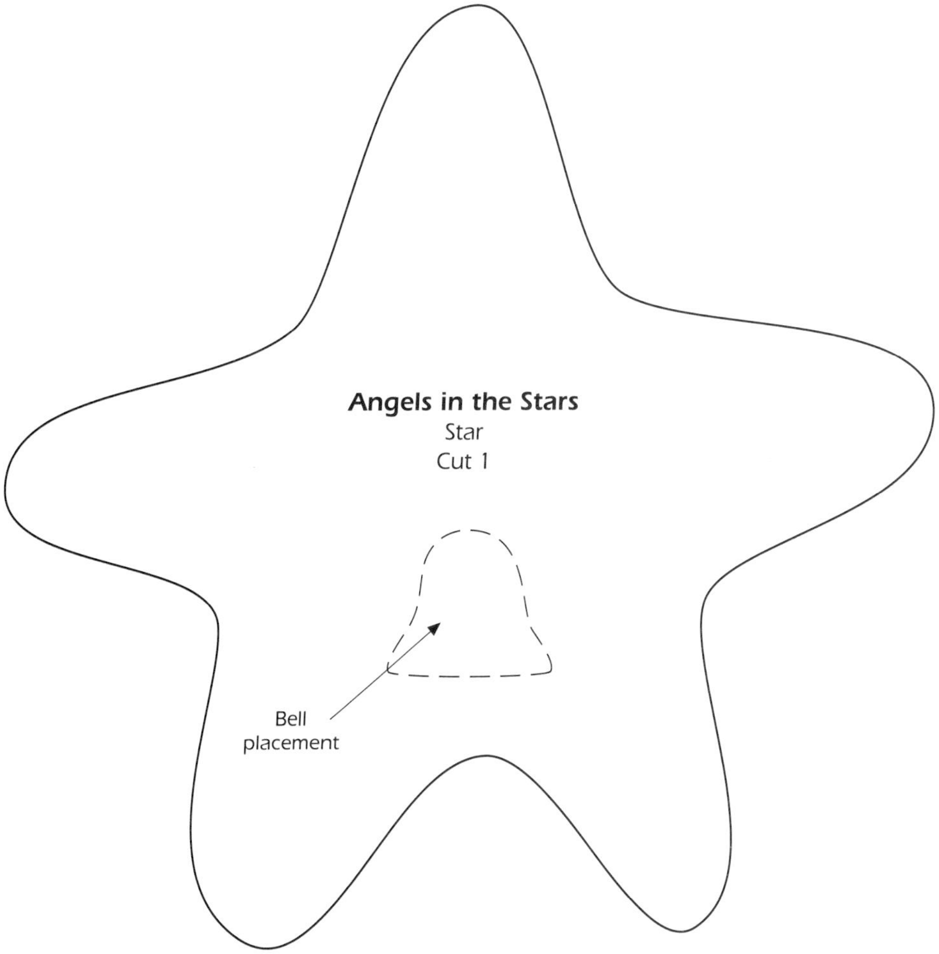

Angels in the Stars
Star
Cut 1

Bell
placement

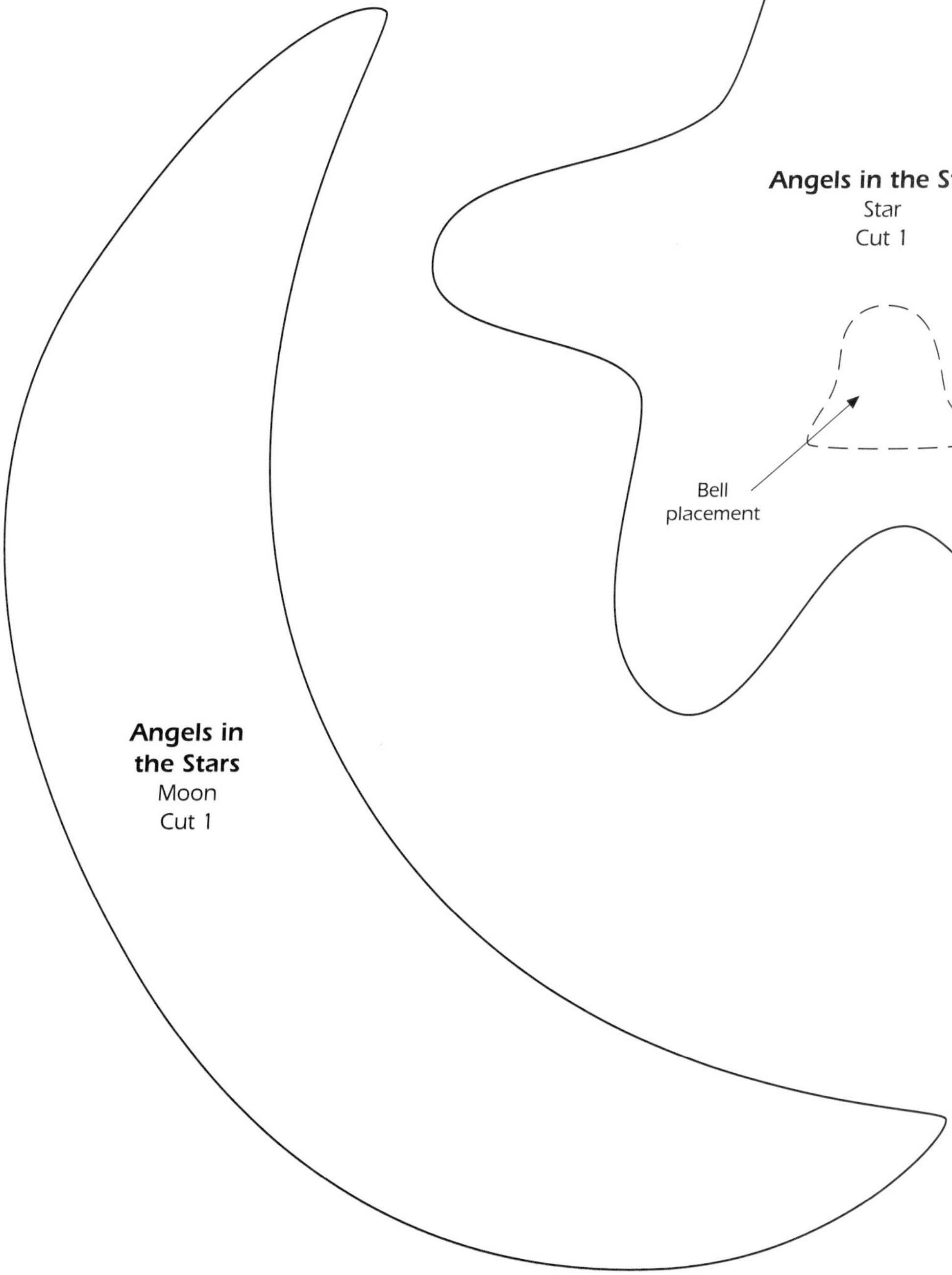

**Angels in
the Stars**
Moon
Cut 1

For the angel templates,
refer to the pullout pattern.

Angel Sampler

*With angels and a wish for peace,
this quilt works all year long.
Raffia wings add a primitive touch.*

Color Photo: page 22
Size: 19½" x 30½"
Materials: 44"-wide fabric

¼ yd. each of 3 prints for background

⅓ yd. plaid for border (If your fabric is 44" wide, you can cut two 3½"-wide strips from ¼ yd.)

⅛ yd. print for binding

25" x 36" piece of fabric for backing

25" x 36" piece of Pellon fleece or other thin batting

⅛ yd. paper-backed fusible web (such as Wonder-Under)

¼ yd. each or scraps of the following:

    2 blue prints for dresses
    Muslin for faces
    White print for wing
    Yellow print for halo
    Tan print for stars
    Blue plaid for letters

Lace for collar, approximately 4" long

Black embroidery floss for hair

#8 perle cotton in assorted colors

Raffia for wings

11 buttons for small stars

5 cinnamon buttons for hair

Making the Foundation
Cutting

From the printed background fabrics, cut:
- 1 rectangle, 8½" x 16½", for Flying Angel block background
- 1 rectangle, 5½" x 16½", for Peace block background
- 1 rectangle, 8½" x 13½", for Standing Angel block background

From the plaid fabric, cut:
- 2 strips, each 3½" x 13½", for side borders
- 2 strips, each 3½" x 30½", for top and bottom borders

From the printed fabric, cut:
- 3 strips, each 1½" x 44", for binding

Assembly

All seams are ¼" wide.

1. Layer the batting on the backing fabric. Smooth the batting and backing, working out from the center. See "Making the Quilt Sandwich Foundation" on page 10.
2. Place the 8½" x 16½" Flying Angel block background on the upper right corner of the batting, 6" down from the top and 6" in from the right side. Pin in place.

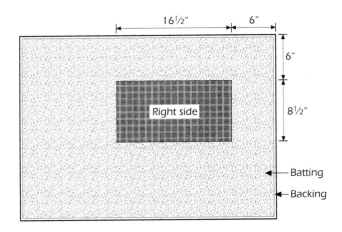

3. Matching the 16½" sides, place the 5½" x 16½" Peace block background on top of the Flying Angel block background, right sides together. Pin in place.

4. Stitch along the top and bottom of the Flying Angel block background.

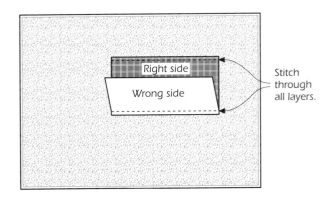

5. Flip the Peace block background onto the batting. Press the seam.
6. Place the 8½" x 13½" Standing Angel block background, right sides together, on top of the unit just sewn. Match the left 13½" sides and pin in place.
7. Stitch along the left side.

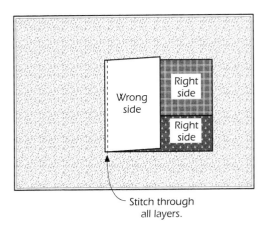

8. Flip the Standing Angel block background onto the batting. Press the seam.
9. Add the side, top, and bottom borders, in that order, as you did the backgrounds. Press the seam after adding each border. Your completed foundation should look like the illustration below.

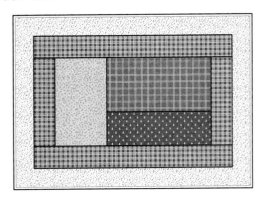

10. Bind the edges with 1½"-wide strips, following the directions on page 13.

Appliquilt

Use the templates on pages 31–32 and on the pullout pattern. Refer to the templates and the quilt plan on page 28 for layout. The numbers on the templates indicate the stitching order.

1. Make plastic templates, following the directions on page 11.
2. Cut out the appliqué pieces, except for the letters, from the fabrics described in the "Materials" list.
3. Stitch the flying angel to the top right background.
4. Cut 10"- to 12"-long pieces of raffia (20 to 25 pieces). Place the raffia in the center of the left background rectangle, approximately 5" down from the top, and stitch. Stitch the angel body and head on top of the raffia.

5. Trace the lettering, as printed, onto the paper side of paper-backed fusible web. Press the traced letters onto wrong side of the blue plaid, following the manufacturer's instructions.
6. Cut out the letters and peel away the paper backing. Place each letter, right side up, in the center of a large star. Press the letters in place.
7. Stitch the large stars to the bottom right rectangle.
8. Stitch the small stars to the quilt.

Embellishments

1. Sew buttons in the center of the stars and on the standing angel's head.
2. Sew the lace to the neckline of the standing angel. Gather the lace as you sew.
3. Using all 6 strands of embroidery floss, make French knots for the flying angel's hair as shown on the templates.

5"

Stitch through all layers.

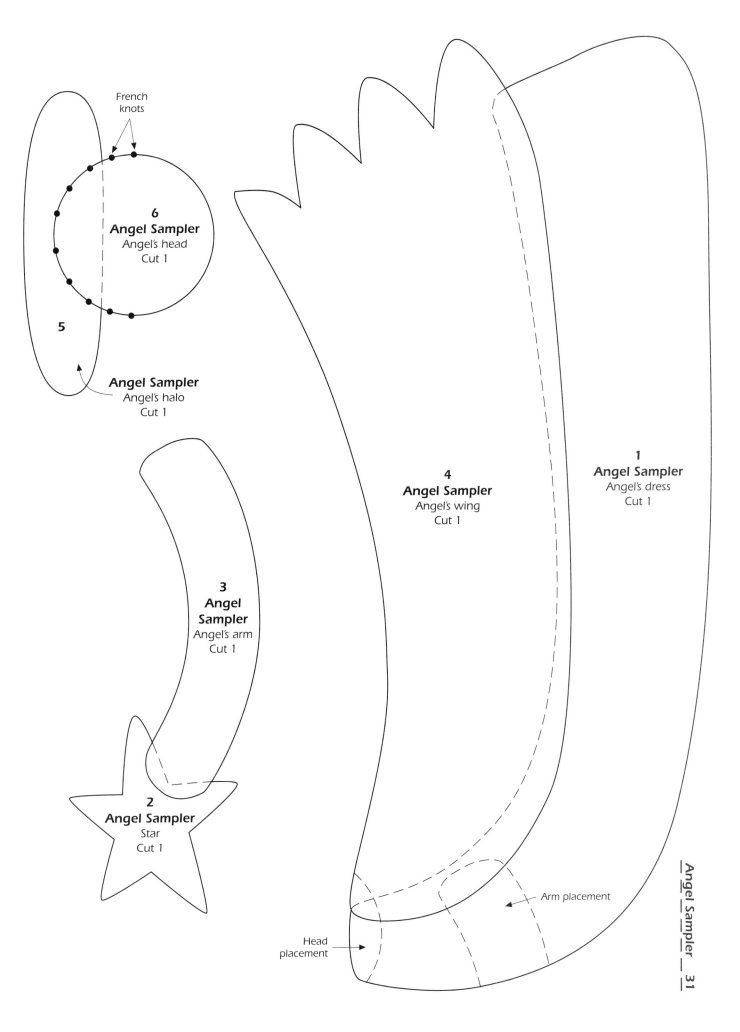

French
knots

6
Angel Sampler
Angel's head
Cut 1

5

Angel Sampler
Angel's halo
Cut 1

4
Angel Sampler
Angel's wing
Cut 1

1
Angel Sampler
Angel's dress
Cut 1

3
Angel
Sampler
Angel's arm
Cut 1

2
Angel Sampler
Star
Cut 1

Arm placement

Head
placement

Angel Sampler
Large star
Cut 5

Angel Sampler
Medium star
Cut 5

Angel Sampler
Small star
Cut 5

For the standing angel template, refer to the pullout pattern.

In the quilt illustration:

Every tree through-out the world bloomed and bore fruit on Christmas Eve

O Christmas Tree

The excerpt included in this quilt is from a tenth-century legend. It was found in Susan Stewart Branch's beautiful book **Christmas from the Heart of the Home**.

A black night sky with metallic stars would give this project a whole other look!

Color Photo: page 22
Size: 17½" x 34"
Materials: 44"-wide fabric

⅜ yd. large-scale check for background

⅛ yd. large-scale plaid for left and top borders

¼ yd. small-scale plaid for right and bottom borders

¼ yd. small-scale check for binding

21" x 38" piece of Pellon fleece or other thin batting

21" x 38" piece of fabric for backing

Scraps:

    ¼ yd. total of 5 prints for trees
    Grunged muslin for verse (see page 7)

Transfer pen

Plain white paper

Green embroidery floss for lettering

#8 perle cotton in assorted colors

34 buttons

Making the Foundation
Cutting

From the large-scale checked fabric, cut:
1 rectangle, 12½" x 29", for background

From the large-scale plaid fabric, cut:
1 strip, 3½" x 12½", for left side border
1 strip, 3½" x 32", for top border

From the small-scale plaid fabric, cut:
1 strip, 2½" x 15½", for right side border
1 strip, 2½" x 34", for bottom border

From the small-scale checked fabric, cut:
3 strips, each 1½" x 44", for binding

Assembly

All seams are ¼" wide.

1. Lay the batting on the backing fabric. Smooth the batting and backing, working out from the center. See "Making the Quilt Sandwich Foundation" on page 10.
2. Place the 12½" x 29" checked background in the center of the batting. Pin in place.
3. With right sides together, pin the 3½" x 12½" plaid strip on the left side of the background.
4. Stitch through all the layers.

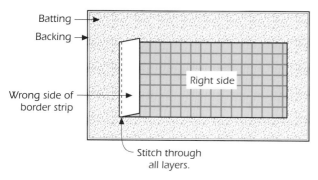

Batting
Backing
Wrong side of border strip
Right side
Stitch through all layers.

5. Flip the border right side up onto the batting. Press the seam.

6. Repeat this procedure for the top, right side, and bottom borders, in that order. Press the seam after adding each border. Your completed foundation should look like the illustration below.

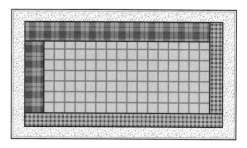

7. Bind the edges with 1½"-wide checked strips, following the directions on page 13.

Appliquilt

Use the templates on the pullout pattern. Refer to the templates and the quilt plan for layout. The numbers on the templates indicate the stitching order.

1. Make plastic templates following the directions on page 11.
2. Cut the appliqué pieces from the fabrics described in the "Materials" list.
3. Using a transfer pen, trace the lettering, as printed, onto a piece of paper.
4. Cut the traced words apart and place, written side down, on the muslin. Press, following the pen manufacturer's instructions. Feel free to arrange the verse however you like.
5. Using 3 strands of embroidery floss, backstitch the lettering on the muslin as shown on page 14.
6. Stitch the trees and muslin to the quilt.

Embellishments

Sew buttons and any other embellishments you like to the quilt. I put moon- and star-shaped buttons above the trees.

Christmas
Dreams

Here's a quilt to appeal to the child in all of us. One of my students, Aiko Kriz, had a photograph of her grandson reproduced on fabric and included him in her quilt (see page 21).
The verse at the bottom of the quilt is from Clement Clarke Moore's **A Visit from St. Nicholas.**

Color Photo: page 20
Size: 30½" x 39½"
Materials: 44"-wide fabric

⅔ yd. check for background

⅜ yd. polka-dot for inner border and binding

½ yd. plaid for outer border

⅓ yd. print for headboard

¼ yd. ticking for pillow

⅓ yd. muslin for cloud and sheet

⅓ yd. flannel to use as backing for cloud and sheet

35" x 45" piece of fabric for backing

35" x 45" piece of Pellon fleece or other thin batting

Scraps:

   ¼ yd. total assorted fabrics for quilt, pajamas, and stockings
   ⅛ yd. total assorted fabrics for faces
   1 strip, 3¼" x 13", linen for verse (optional)

Black and green embroidery floss for hair and lettering

Yellow #3 perle cotton and/or wool or embroidery floss for blond hair and tying quilt

#8 perle cotton in assorted colors

Black buttons for hair

Buttons for pajamas and nightcap

Wooden hearts for headboard

Transfer pen

Plain white paper

⅔ yd. of ½"-wide red ribbon

3" square of paper-backed fusible web (such as Wonder-Under)

Embellishments of your choice, such as miniature toys, bells, and candy canes

Making the Foundation
Cutting

From the checked fabric, cut:
    1 rectangle, 22½" x 31½", for background

From the polka-dot fabric, cut:
    2 strips, 1½" x 31½", for side borders
    2 strips, 1½" x 24½", for top and bottom
        borders

From the plaid fabric, cut:
    2 strips, 3½" x 33½", for side borders
    2 strips, 3½" x 30½", for top and bottom
        borders

Assembly

All seams are ¼" wide.

1. With right sides together, sew the polka-dot inner side border strips to the 22½" x 31½" background. Press the seams.

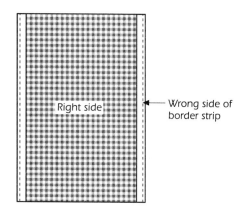

Right side

Wrong side of border strip

2. With right sides together, sew the polka-dot inner top and bottom border strips in place. Press the seams.

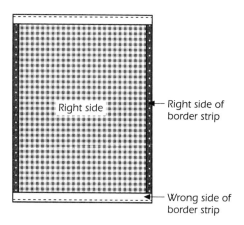

Right side

Right side of border strip

Wrong side of border strip

3. Repeat this procedure for the sides, top, and bottom plaid outer-border strips. Press the seam after adding each border.
4. Layer the top, batting, and backing; baste. See "Making the Quilt Sandwich Foundation" on page 10.

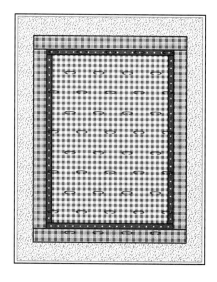

5. Machine or hand quilt in-the-ditch around the inner and outer borders.
6. Bind the edges with 1½"-wide polka-dot strips, following the directions on page 13.

Appliquilt

Use the templates on the pullout pattern and on pages 38–39. Refer to the templates and the quilt plan on page 35 for placement. The numbers on the templates indicate the stitching order.

1. Make plastic templates for the cloud, headboard, pillow, children, sheet, quilt, and Christmas stocking.
2. Cut out the headboard and pillow from the fabrics described in the "Materials" list.
3. Make a loop and tie a bow in the ribbon. Before stitching the headboard in place, slip the loop of ribbon over the bedpost. Stitch the headboard in place.
4. Using pinking shears, cut out the cloud from the muslin. Using straight scissors, cut another cloud, about ⅛" smaller than the template, from the flannel. Place the flannel under the muslin and stitch both to the background. The flannel adds dimension to the cloud and prevents the background fabric from showing through the muslin.
5. Stitch the pillow and children in place. Stitch the nightcap on the middle child.

6. From your scrap fabric, cut twenty-four 4" squares of fabric for the children's quilt. Sew the squares into 6 rows, following the illustration below.

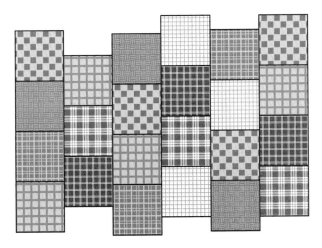

7. Place the quilt template on the wrong side of the pieced top. Remember to reverse the template. Align the dashed lines on the template with the seams. Draw a line around the template and cut out on the line with pinking shears. Stitch the quilt in place. Using #8 perle cotton, tie the quilt as shown on the template.
8. Using pinking shears, cut out the sheet from the muslin. Using straight scissors, cut another sheet, about ⅛" smaller than the template, from the flannel. Place this under the muslin piece. With right sides together, place both the muslin and flannel sheet pieces below the children. Machine stitch the sheet to the top of the children's quilt.

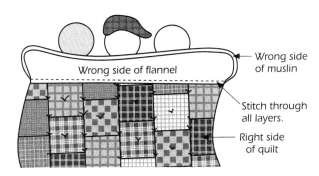

Wrong side of flannel

Wrong side of muslin

Stitch through all layers.

Right side of quilt

9. Flip the sheet down over the top of the children's quilt. Press. Appliquilt the sheet along the remaining free edges.

Embellishments

Referring to the quilt plan and photo for placement, sew on buttons and other embellishments.

Stocking

1. Make a plastic template for the stocking.
2. Place the stocking template on 2 pieces of fabric, right sides together. Trace around the template with a pencil. Cut out the stockings ¼" outside the drawn line.
3. With right sides together, stitch the pieces together on the drawn line. Leave the top of the stocking open. Turn right side out and press.
4. Reverse the toe, heel, and heart templates and trace on paper-backed fusible web. Press the traced pieces onto the wrong side of the fabric, following the manufacturer's instructions. Cut out the pieces and peel away the paper backing. Place the pieces, right sides up, on the stocking. Press.
5. To attach the stocking to the headboard, position the stocking on the ribbon (refer to the quilt photo for placement). Sew the button to the top corner of the stocking, stitching through the ribbon.

Children

1. Using 3 strands of black embroidery floss, backstitch to make closed eyelids, following the lines on the template. See "Adding Embellishments" on page 14.
2. Using 6 strands of black embroidery floss, sew black buttons to the right-hand child's head as shown on the template. Cut the ends of the floss to about 1½" and separate the strands.
3. Cut 4"-long pieces of yellow wool, perle cotton, or embroidery floss. Stitch the center of the lengths to the edge of the left-hand child's head.

Using a 6"-long piece of perle cotton or embroidery floss, stitch through the quilt to the edge of the girl's head. Tie a bow ½" from the edge of her head to hold the ends of the hair in place.

Verse

1. Using a transfer pen, trace the verse, as printed on page 39, onto a piece of paper. Transfer to linen, following the pen manufacturer's instructions.
2. Backstitch, using 3 strands of green embroidery floss.
3. Appliquilt the linen piece to the bottom of the quilt. Fray the edges of the fabric by gently removing threads from each edge.

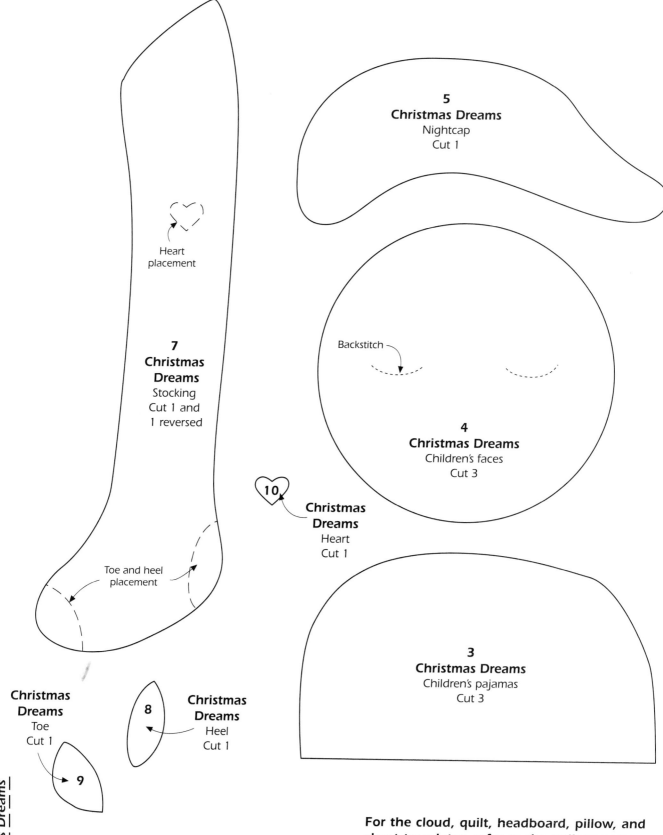

5
Christmas Dreams
Nightcap
Cut 1

Heart
placement

Backstitch

7
**Christmas
Dreams**
Stocking
Cut 1 and
1 reversed

4
Christmas Dreams
Children's faces
Cut 3

10
**Christmas
Dreams**
Heart
Cut 1

Toe and heel
placement

3
Christmas Dreams
Children's pajamas
Cut 3

**Christmas
Dreams**
Toe
Cut 1

8

**Christmas
Dreams**
Heel
Cut 1

9

For the cloud, quilt, headboard, pillow, and
sheet templates, refer to the pullout pattern.

di) nnain their beds
the children were
all xmas eve (nestled)

Yo-Yo Christmas

You'll find these yo-yos quick and easy to make. The patchwork border makes it a real country Christmas.

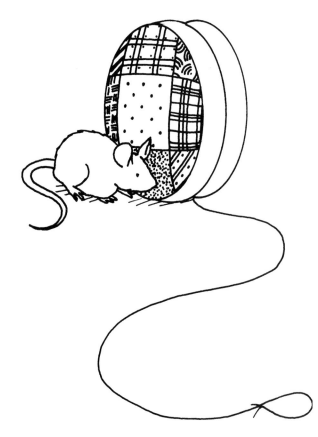

Color Photo: page 18
Size: 26" x 26"
Materials: 44"-wide fabric

³⁄₈ yd. plaid for background

1 yd. total of 8 fabrics for borders, lattice (sashing between the blocks), and yo-yos

¼ yd. print for binding

29" x 29" piece of fabric for backing

29" x 29" piece of Pellon fleece or other thin batting

Burlap for tree base

#8 perle cotton in assorted colors

Raffia for wreath

Embellishments of your choice, such as cinnamon buttons, round buttons, dried flowers, and tin heart or other ornament

Making the Foundation
Cutting

From the plaid fabric, cut:
   1 rectangle, 12½" x 20", for Tree block background
   1 rectangle, 6½" x 8", for Wreath block background
   1 rectangle, 6½" x 11", for Stocking block background

From the 8 fabrics, cut:
   1 strip, 2" x 44", of each for borders and lattice
   9 squares, 2" x 2", for borders and lattice

From the printed fabric, cut:
   3 strips, each 1½" x 44", for binding

Assembly

All seams are ¼" wide.

1. Divide the eight 2" x 44" strips into 2 groups of 4 strips each. Join the strips, pressing the seams to one side. Cut thirty-two 2" x 6½" units. Set aside.

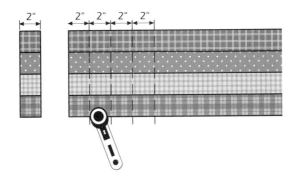

2. Layer the batting on the backing fabric, matching the edges. Smooth the batting and backing, working out from the center.
3. Place the 12½" x 20" Tree block background on the left side of the batting, 5" down from the top and 5" in from the left side. Pin in place.
4. Stitch one 2" x 6½" unit to the bottom of the 6½" x 8" Wreath block background. Stitch the 6½" x 11" Stocking block background to the bottom of the lattice. Press the seams. Set this unit aside.
5. To make the vertical lattice strip, stitch three 2" x 6½" units together, end to end. Stitch a 2" square to one end. The finished lattice strip should have 13 squares. Press the seams.

6. Lay this lattice strip on the right edge of the 12½" x 20" background, right sides together. Stitch through all the layers. Flip the lattice strip right side up onto the batting. Press the seam.

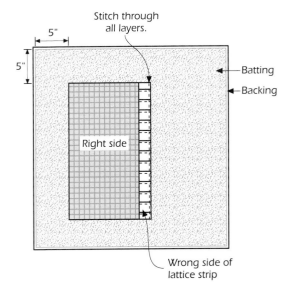

7. Lay the background-block unit constructed in step 4 on the right side of the vertical lattice strip, right sides together. Stitch through all the layers. Flip the block set right side up onto the batting. Press the seam.
8. To make the left side border, stitch two 2" x 6½" units together on the long side. Make 2 more of these 3½" x 6½" sets. Press the seams.

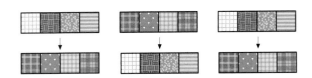

Stitch these sets together on the short side. Press the seams.

Stitch two 2" squares together. Press the seam. Stitch this unit to one end of the patchwork border.

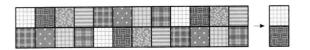

9. Repeat step 8 to make the right side border. Both borders should measure 3½" x 20".
10. With right sides together, pin the patchwork borders to the sides of the finished background. Stitch through all the layers. Flip the borders right side up onto the batting. Press the seams.
11. To make the top and bottom borders, repeat step 8, using eight 2" x 6½" units and two 2" squares for each border.
12. With right sides together, pin the pieced border strips to the top and bottom of the background. Stitch through all the layers. Flip the borders right side up onto the batting. Press the seams. Your completed foundation should look like the illustration below.

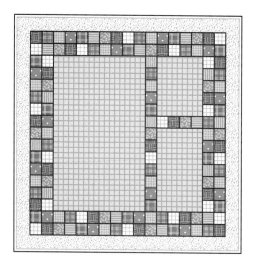

13. Bind the edges with 1½"-wide strips, following the directions on page 13. Because of the number of seams and the stretchiness of your fabrics, your patchwork borders may not fit the background precisely. It's okay to add a partial square here or there or to trim a square if necessary. The unevenness adds to the primitive or "patched" look, which I find charming.

   I really want everyone to enjoy these projects and not "stress out" over unmatched seams; it just doesn't matter. Check out the size of some of the blocks in my quilt on page 18.

Appliquilt

Use the templates on page 43. Refer to the templates and the quilt plan on page 40 for layout. The numbers on the templates indicate the stitching order.
1. Make plastic templates, following the directions on page 11.
2. Cut the appliqué pieces from the fabrics described in the "Materials" list.
3. Stitch the cuff, heel, and toe to the stocking, then stitch the stocking to the quilt. Do not stitch the top of the stocking to the quilt.
4. Stitch the tree base in place.
5. Using the 8 assorted fabrics, make 26 yo-yos as shown on page 15. As you make each yo-yo, stitch it to the quilt with a button. Refer to the illustration for placement.

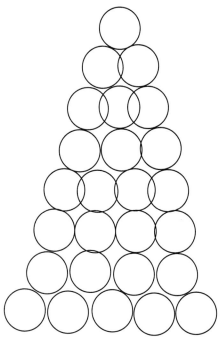

Yo-Yo Placement

6. To make the wreath, wind 8 strands of raffia into a circle approximately 5" in diameter. Tie with strips of torn fabric (approximately 1" x 4") at 3 evenly spaced points. Stitch in place.

Embellishments

1. Attach the tin heart or another ornament to the wreath with perle cotton or embroidery floss.
2. Sew the buttons randomly on the patchwork borders and stocking. Sew the cinnamon buttons on the Tree block.
3. Place dried flowers, candy canes, or ornaments in the stocking.

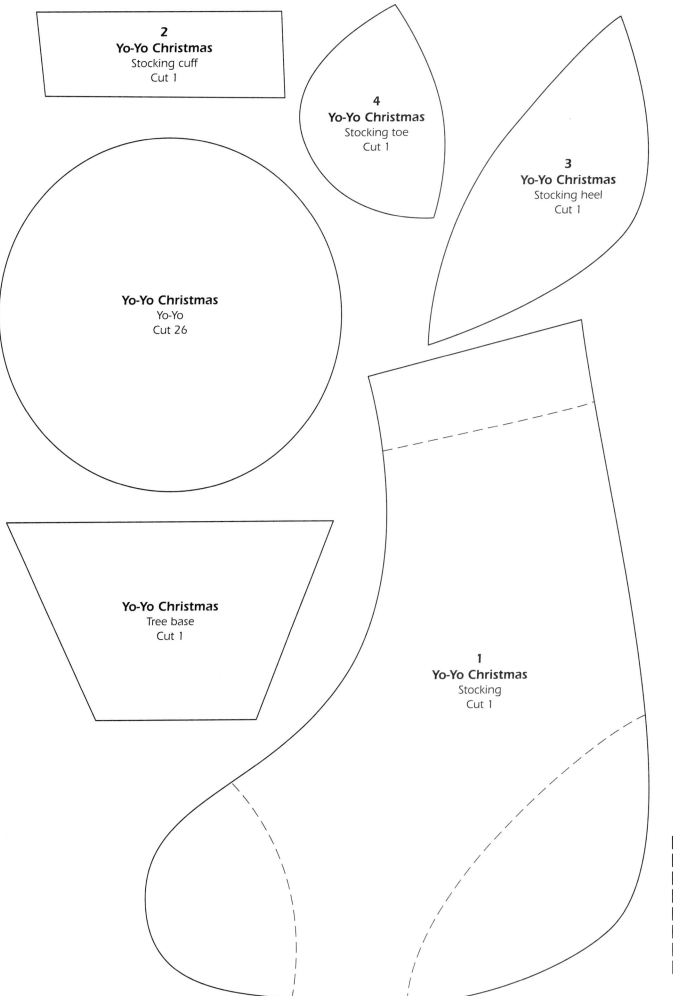

2
Yo-Yo Christmas
Stocking cuff
Cut 1

4
Yo-Yo Christmas
Stocking toe
Cut 1

3
Yo-Yo Christmas
Stocking heel
Cut 1

Yo-Yo Christmas
Yo-Yo
Cut 26

Yo-Yo Christmas
Tree base
Cut 1

1
Yo-Yo Christmas
Stocking
Cut 1

Favorite Things

A simple sampler of my favorite things.
Add a few of your own to make this quilt a
work of "heart" for you and yours!

Color Photo: page 17
Size: 38½" x 41½"
Materials: 44"-wide fabric

1⅜ yds. total of 6 prints for background

¼ yd. red print for left and top borders

¼ yd. green print for right and bottom borders

¼ yd. print for binding or scraps

45" x 47" piece of fabric for backing

45" x 47" piece of Pellon fleece or other thin batting

¼ yd. each or scraps of the following:
   4 browns for stars
   6 reds for dresses and pinafores
   3 fabrics for faces and hands
   2 tans for gingerbread men
   4 greens for trees
   4 dark browns for tree trunks
   1 red print for bells
   1 green print for bells

Jute in assorted weights for bells

2 lace doilies for angels' wings

Gold embroidery floss for angels' halos

#8 perle cotton in assorted colors

Embellishments of your choice, such as small heart buttons, round buttons, and bells

Making the Foundation
Cutting

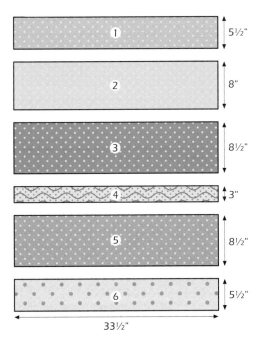

**Favorite Things
Cutting Plan**

The background strips are numbered from top to bottom. Arrange the strips in order, referring to the Favorite Things Cutting Plan above. You may want to pin numbered pieces of paper to each strip to help you during assembly.

From the 6 printed fabrics, cut:
1 strip, 5½" x 33½", for Background 1
1 strip, 8" x 33½", for Background 2
1 strip, 8½" x 33½", for Background 3
1 strip, 3" x 33½", for Background 4
1 strip, 8½" x 33½", for Background 5
1 strip, 5½" x 33½", for Background 6

From the red fabric, cut:
1 strip, 2½" x 38½", for left border
1 strip, 3½" x 38½", for top border

From the green fabric, cut:
1 strip, 3½" x 36½", for right border
1 strip, 2½" x 36½", for bottom border

Assembly

All seams are ¼" wide.

1. Layer the batting on the backing fabric. Smooth the batting and backing, working out from the center. See "Making the Quilt Sandwich Foundation" on page 10.
2. Place Background 1, right side up, 6½" down from the top and 4½" in from the left side of the batting. Pin in place.

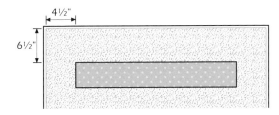

3. Place Background 2 on top of Background 1, right sides together. Align the bottom edges, pinning in place. Stitch along the bottom edge.
4. Flip Background 2 right side up onto the batting. Press the seam.
5. Repeat steps 3 and 4 for the remaining background strips. Press each new seam well so the quilt will hang straight and flat.
6. With right sides together, pin the right border strip on the pieced background. Line up the right edges. Stitch through all the layers.

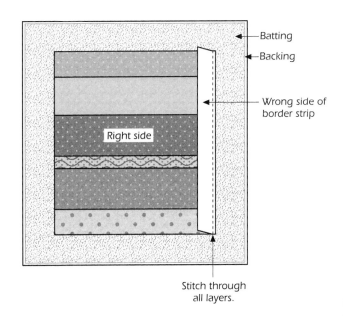

7. Flip the right border strip onto the batting. Press the seam.

8. Repeat steps 6 and 7 for the bottom, left, and top borders, in that order. Press the new seam after adding each border. Your completed foundation should look like the illustration below.

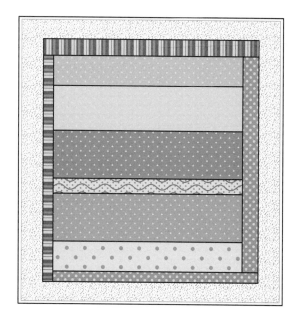

9. Trim the batting and backing even with the edges. To make the binding, cut 1½"-wide strips from the ¼ yard of printed fabric or scraps. If using scraps, cut the strips in varying lengths. I used a traditional binding for my quilt. You can use the method described on page 13 or your favorite traditional binding method.

Appliquilt

Use the templates on pages 47–49. Refer to the templates and the quilt plan on page 44 for layout. The numbers on the templates indicate the stitching order.

1. Make plastic templates, following the directions on page 11.
2. Cut the appliqué pieces from the fabrics described in the "Materials" list.
3. Stitch the stars, gingerbread men, trees, and bells to the background. Cut the lace doilies in half or in a place where you have ½" to tuck under the angels' pinafores. Stitch the angels to the background, pinning each doily in place and stitching the pinafores over the lower edges.

Embellishments

1. Sew buttons along the top of the doilies to secure.
2. Sew a button in the center of each star.
3. Using a backstitch, embroider halos with 3 strands of gold embroidery floss.
4. Sew small heart buttons on the gingerbread men.
5. Sew assorted buttons to decorate the Christmas trees. Sew a star button at the top of each tree.
6. Sew a small bell at the bottom of each appliqué bell.
7. Cut 12" lengths of various weights of jute. Sew a piece of jute to the top of each appliqué bell. Trim the ends.

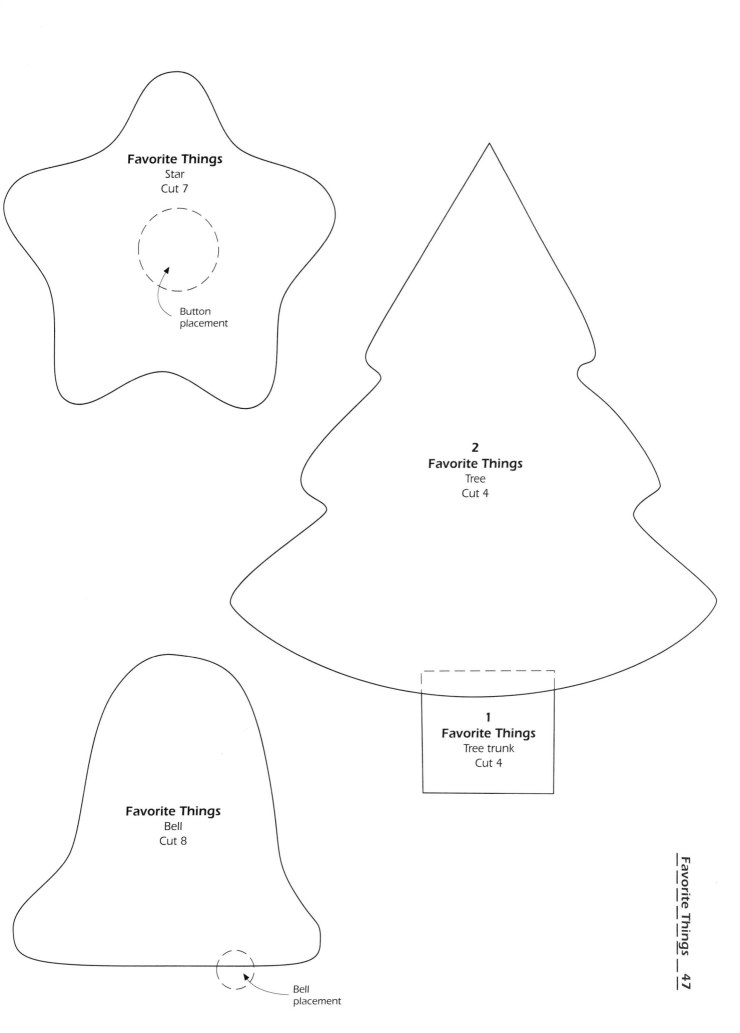

Favorite Things
Star
Cut 7

Button
placement

2
Favorite Things
Tree
Cut 4

1
Favorite Things
Tree trunk
Cut 4

Favorite Things
Bell
Cut 8

Bell
placement

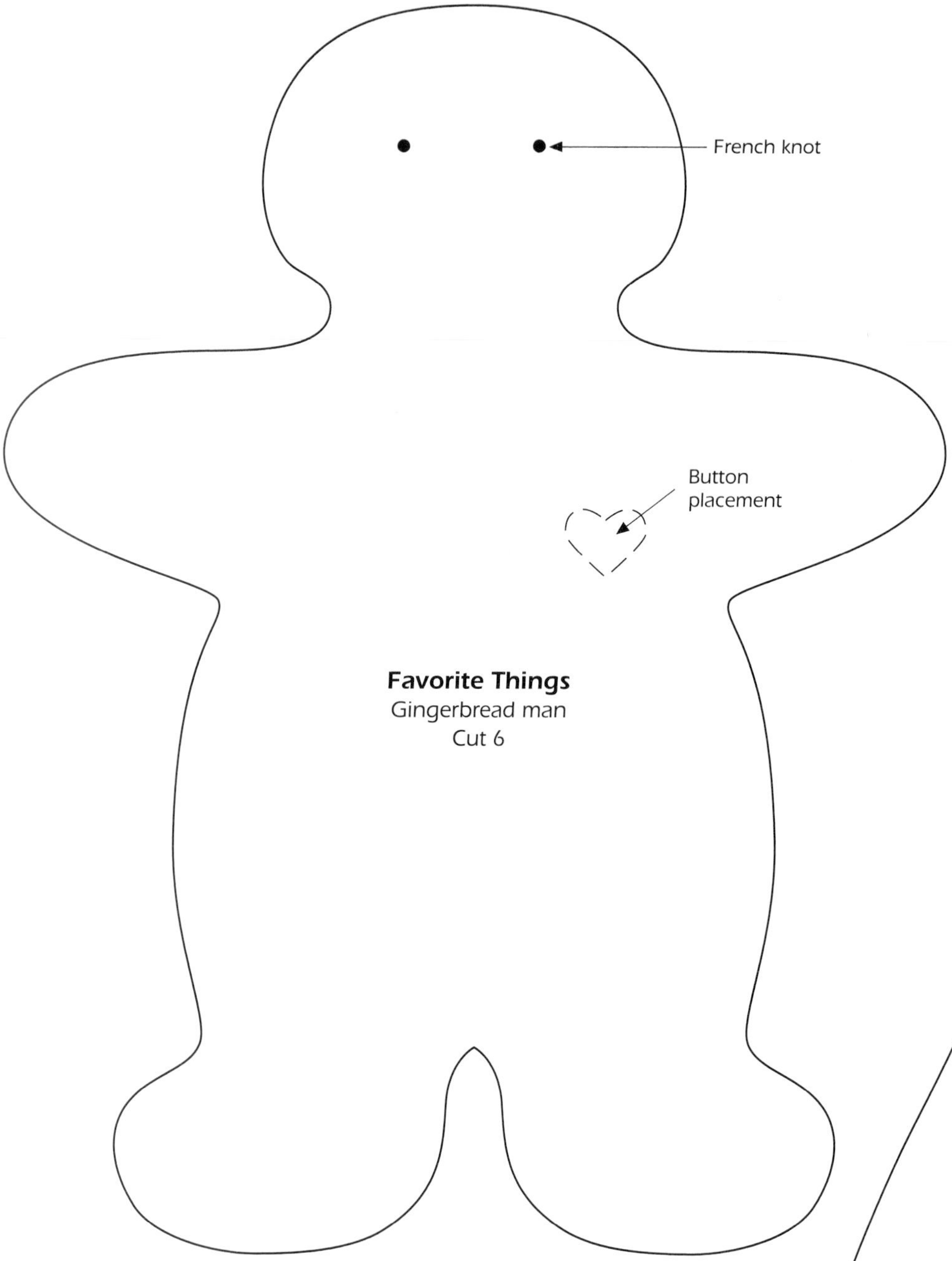

French knot

Button
placement

Favorite Things
Gingerbread man
Cut 6

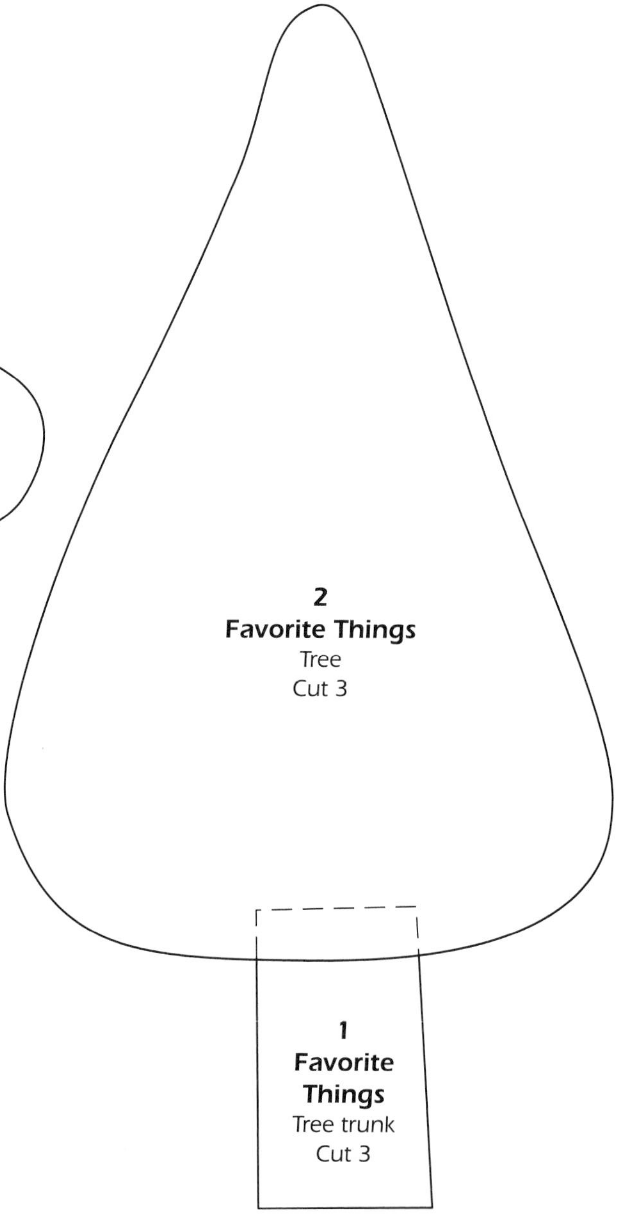

2
Favorite Things
Tree
Cut 3

1
Favorite Things
Tree trunk
Cut 3

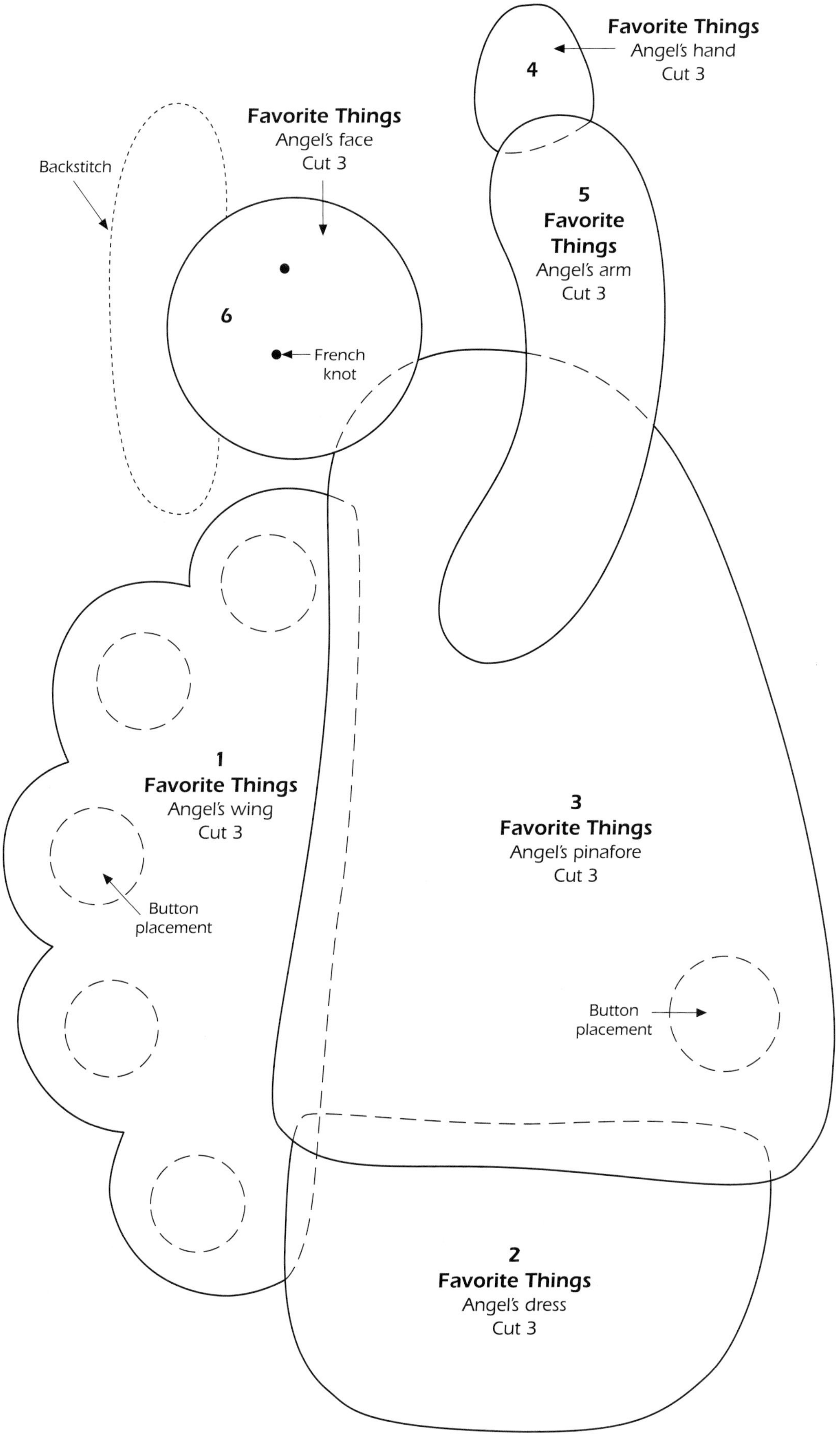

Favorite Things
Angel's hand
Cut 3

4

5
Favorite Things
Angel's arm
Cut 3

Backstitch

Favorite Things
Angel's face
Cut 3

6

French knot

1
Favorite Things
Angel's wing
Cut 3

Button placement

3
Favorite Things
Angel's pinafore
Cut 3

Button placement

2
Favorite Things
Angel's dress
Cut 3

Christmas Goose

This quilt would be great in the dining room or in Dad's den with a masculine plaid tie and wooden beads for berries.

Color Photo: page 21
Size: 26" x 22½"
Materials: 44"-wide fabric

½ yd. (or fat quarter) yellow check for background

⅓ yd. yellow plaid for left and top borders and binding

⅛ yd. yellow stripe for right border

⅛ yd. black plaid for bottom border

28" x 30" piece of fabric for backing

28" x 30" piece of Pellon fleece or other thin batting

⅛ to ¼ yd. each or scraps of the following:

> 2 dark yellows for goose body
> Beige for goose body
> Dark gray for goose neck
> Red stripe for ribbon
> 5 green prints for leaves

#8 perle cotton in assorted colors

13 buttons or beads for goose's eye, berries, and ribbon

Making the Foundation
Cutting

From the yellow checked fabric, cut:
1 rectangle, 18" x 21", for background

From the yellow plaid fabric, cut:
1 strip, 2½" x 20", for left border
1 strip, 3" x 26", for top border
2 strips, 1½" x 44", for binding
1 strip, 1½" x 15", for binding

From the yellow striped fabric, cut:
1 strip, 3½" x 18", for right border

From the black plaid, cut:
1 strip, 2½" x 24", for bottom border

Assembly

All seams are ¼" wide.

1. Layer the batting on the backing fabric. Smooth the batting and backing, working out from the center. See "Making the Quilt Sandwich Foundation" on page 10.
2. Place the 18" x 21" background in the center of the batting.
3. With right sides together, pin the striped 3½" x 18" strip to the right edge of the background. Stitch through all the layers.

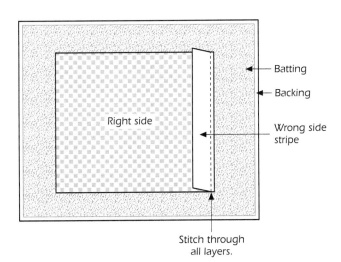

Batting
Backing
Right side
Wrong side stripe
Stitch through all layers.

4. Flip the border strip right side up onto the batting. Press the seam.

5. Repeat steps 3 and 4 for the bottom, left, and top borders, in that order. Press the new seam after adding each border. Your completed foundation should look like the illustration below.

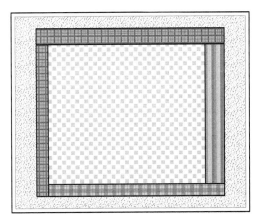

6. Bind the edges with 1½"-wide yellow plaid strips, following the directions on page 13.

Appliquilt

Use the templates on the pullout pattern. Refer to the templates and the quilt plan on page 50 for layout. The numbers on the templates indicate the stitching order.

1. Make plastic templates following the directions on page 11.
2. Cut the appliqué pieces from the fabrics described in the "Materials" list.
3. Arrange the four goose pieces in the center of the background.
4. To make the ribbon, cut 1 strip, 2" x 44", from the red stripe. Place the strip behind the goose's neck. Pin the goose's neck on top. Tie a bow and adjust the ends. Pin the ends of the bow out of your way.
5. Stitch the goose pieces in place.
6. Arrange the leaves along the lower edge of the goose and pin in place. To create contrast, place leaves cut from different fabrics next to each other.

Embellishments

1. Secure the ribbon ends with buttons.
2. Sew on a button for the goose's eye.
3. Sew buttons or beads in the leaves for berries.

I ♥ Gingerbread

Here's the fixin's for great decorating, for the holiday or year 'round.

Color Photo: page 24
Size: 18" x 28"
Materials: 44"-wide fabric

Tea towel or ⅝ yd. fabric for background

22" x 32" piece of Pellon fleece or other thin batting

22" x 32" piece of fabric for backing

¼ yd. each or scraps of the following:

> Coordinated colors for letters, heart, oven mitt, and small tea towel
> Brown and/or dark yellow for spice jars
> Beige for jar lids and egg
> Gray for cookie sheet
> Muslin for labels, flour sack, and eggs
> Dark beige and blue fabrics for mixing bowl and sugar sack
> Dark brown for spoon

Transfer pen

Plain white paper

Embellishments of your choice, such as cinnamon buttons, red beads, cookie cutters, and miniature rolling pin

FIMO® modeling clay for gingerbread man

Small amount of Poly-Fil™ or other stuffing

Making the Foundation
Cutting

From the background fabric, cut:

1 rectangle, 20" x 30", as an alternative to a tea towel

Assembly

1. Layer the batting on the backing fabric. Smooth the batting and backing, working out from the center. See "Making the Quilt Sandwich Foundation" on page 10.
2. If you're using a piece of fabric for the background, rather than a tea towel, hem the edges. Using a ¼"-wide seam allowance, turn the edges under twice toward the wrong side of fabric. Stitch the edges. Press the seams.

3. Using a ruler and pencil, draw a grid of squares on the fabric. I suggest drawing single lines 2½" apart. The grid on the tea towel I used has two lines.
4. Place the fabric background or tea towel in the center of the batting. Following the instructions on page 10, pin baste as shown.

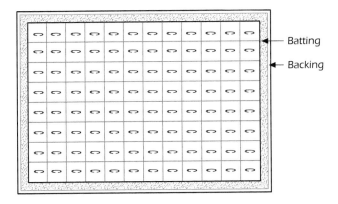

5. If you've made a fabric background, stitch on the pencil lines. If you're using a tea towel with double lines, stitch between the lines. You can remove the pins as you stitch or after you complete the quilting.
6. Using pinking shears or the pinking blade of a rotary cutter, trim the excess fleece and backing even with the edges of the top.

Appliquilt

Use the templates and transfer lettering on pages 55–56 and on the pullout pattern. Refer to the templates and the quilt plan on page 52 for layout. The numbers on the templates indicate the stitching order.

1. Make plastic templates, following the directions on page 11.
2. **Mixing bowl.** To piece the bowl, cut 1 strip, 2" x 6", and 1 strip, 2½" x 6", from the beige fabric. Cut 1 strip, 1" x 6", from the blue fabric. With right sides together, stitch the 2" x 6" beige strip to the 1" x 6" blue strip along the 6" side. Next, stitch the 2½" x 6" beige strip to the right side of the blue strip. Press the seams. Place the bowl template on the wrong side of the pieced fabric rectangle and trace around the template. Using pinking shears, cut out the bowl. Stitch in place.
3. **Flour and sugar sacks.** From the muslin, cut a 1" x 2" rectangle for the sugar sack label. Using a transfer pen, trace "FLOUR" and "SUGAR" onto plain white paper. Place the paper face down on the fabric for the flour sack and sugar label. Iron the lettering onto the fabric, following the manufacturer's directions. You can also use a black permanent-ink marker to write the words on the fabric.

   To make the flour and sugar sacks, cut 1 strip, 3" x 9", from the muslin and the dark beige fabrics. Fold each 3" x 9" piece in half, right sides together, and stitch along the 4½" sides. Turn right side out and press.

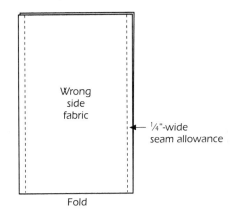

Tie a knot in the thread, leaving a 6"-long tail. Beginning on the front of each bag, about 1" down from the top, stitch around the top of the bag. Stitch the back of each bag to the quilt top. Fill each bag with a small amount of stuffing. Gather the top of each bag slightly. Knot the thread ends and trim.

Stitching

Stitch back of bag to quilt top.

4. **Spice jar labels.** Cut 2 rectangles, each 1¼" x 2", from the muslin. Use the transfer process described in step 3 to make the labels.

5. **Oven mitt.** Place the template on the fold of fabric and trace around the entire template. Open the mitt. Turn under a ¼"-hem on the bottom of the mitt toward the wrong side of the fabric. Stitch in place. Fold the mitt in half, wrong

sides together, and match the edges. Stitch the mitt together using a ⅛"-wide seam allowance. Clip the curves, then turn right side out. Press. Stitch only the back of the oven mitt to the background.

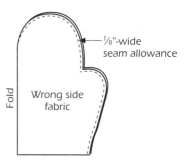

⅛"-wide seam allowance

Fold

Wrong side fabric

6. **Tea towel.** Cut a 4" x 7" rectangle from the fabric described in the "Materials" list. Using a ¼"-wide seam allowance, turn the edges of the rectangle under twice toward the wrong side of the fabric. Stitch the edges. Press the seams.

   Referring to the quilt plan on page 52 and the quilt photo on page 24, arrange the tea towel and pin in place. Referring to "Adding Embellishments" on page 14, attach the rolling pin on top of the tea towel. Attach the tea towel by taking one stitch from the back of the quilt where pinned.

7. **Gingerbread man.** Read the modeling clay manufacturer's instructions completely. Roll out the clay to a ¼" thickness. Place the template on top of the clay, then trace around the template with a toothpick. Remove the template and, using a sharp knife, cut out the gingerbread man. Remove the excess clay. Press red beads into the clay. Using a toothpick, make holes where indicated on the template. Bake your gingerbread man with the red beads, according to the manufacturer's instructions.

   Attach the gingerbread man as you would sew on a button, stitching through the holes made before baking.

8. **Letters.** Cut the appliqué pieces from the fabric described in the "Materials" list. Stitch in place, referring to the quilt plan on page 52 for placement.

Embellishments

1. When stitching cinnamon gingerbread buttons to the cookie sheet, attach a tiny red bead to each hole and sew in place, sewing each hole separately.

2. Stitch a cookie cutter and small red beads around the baking pan.

I ❤ **Gingerbread**
Cookie sheet
Cut 1

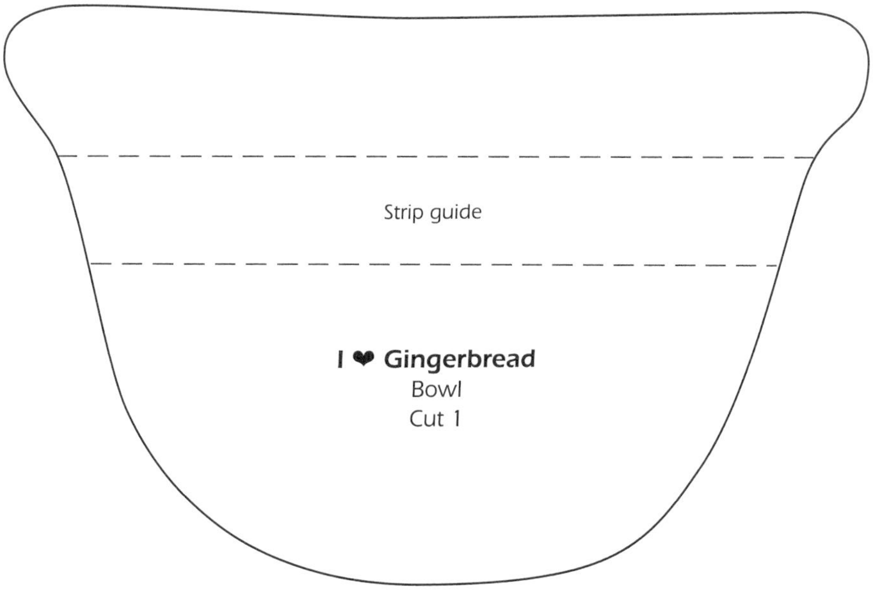

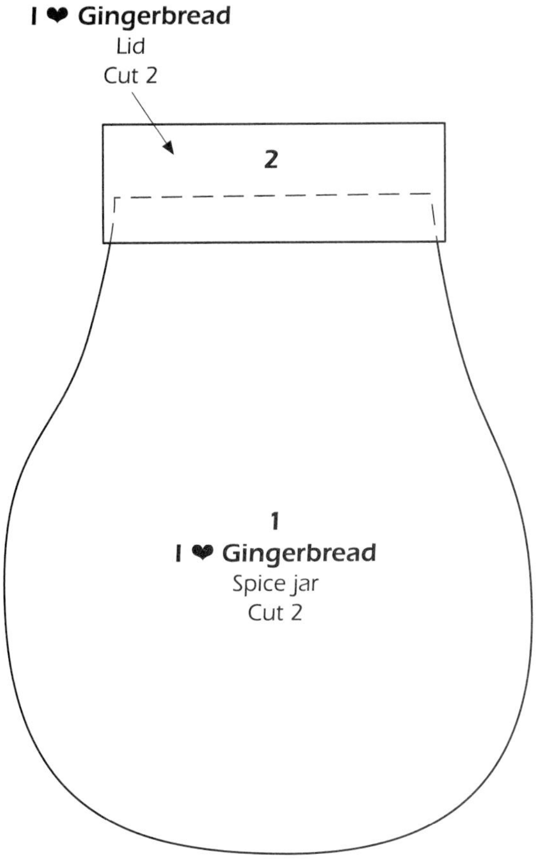

I ❤ **Gingerbread**
Lid
Cut 2

2

Strip guide

I ❤ **Gingerbread**
Bowl
Cut 1

1
I ❤ **Gingerbread**
Spice jar
Cut 2

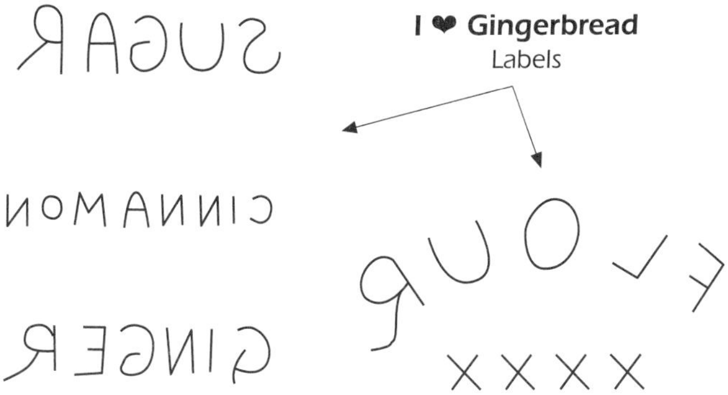

ЯAƏUꙄ

CINNAMON

ЯƎƆNIƆ

I ❤ **Gingerbread**
Labels

FLOUꓤ

xxxx

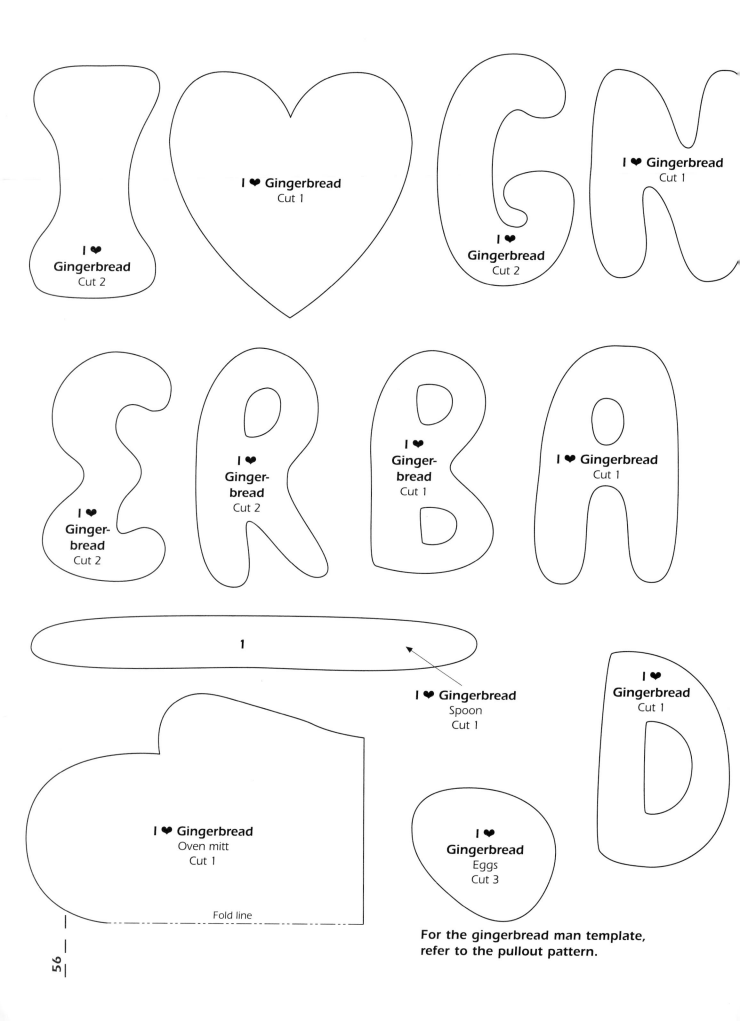

I ❤ Gingerbread
Cut 2

I ❤ Gingerbread
Cut 1

I ❤ Gingerbread
Cut 1

I ❤ Gingerbread
Cut 2

I ❤ Gingerbread
Cut 2

I ❤ Ginger-bread
Cut 2

I ❤ Ginger-bread
Cut 1

I ❤ Gingerbread
Cut 1

1

I ❤ Gingerbread
Spoon
Cut 1

I ❤ Gingerbread
Cut 1

I ❤ Gingerbread
Oven mitt
Cut 1

Fold line

I ❤ Gingerbread
Eggs
Cut 3

For the gingerbread man template,
refer to the pullout pattern.

Christmas Joy

*Use this quilted wall hanging to
spell out the joy of the season,
or display each letter separately.
This is a great opportunity to use
fat-quarter packets!*

Color Photo: page 24
Size: Each piece is approximately 11" x 17"
Materials: 44"-wide fabric

⅓ yd. red ticking for stocking

⅓ yd. green for wreath

¼ yd. brown for reindeer head

¼ yd. muslin for blaze and antlers

½ yd. muslin or assorted fabrics for backing

½ yd. Pellon fleece or other thin batting

Scraps:

⅔ yd. total assorted greens for yo-yos
⅛ yd. total assorted reds and greens for heel,
   toe, cuff, tree, halter, and leaf
⅛ yd. red plaid for ribbon

#8 perle cotton in assorted colors

Embellishments of your choice, such as buttons,
   red beads, snaps, tin or wooden stars, and
   ornaments

Jute

Making the Foundation
Cutting

From the red ticking fabric, cut:
  1 rectangle, 14" x 18", for stocking background

From the green fabric, cut:
  1 rectangle, 14" x 18", for wreath background

From the brown fabric, cut:
  1 rectangle, 8" x 10", for reindeer head

From the muslin fabric, cut:
  1 rectangle, 8" x 10", for blaze
  2 rectangles, each 5" x 10", for antlers

From the backing fabric, cut:
  3 rectangles, each 14" x 18"

From the batting, cut:
  3 rectangles, each 14" x 18"

Assembly
Stocking

1. Layer the batting on the backing fabric. Smooth the batting and backing, working out from the center. See "Making the Quilt Sandwich Foundation" on page 10.
2. Make a plastic template for the stocking, following the directions on page 11. Trace the template onto the right side of the 14" x 18" red stocking background. Do not cut yet.
3. Pin this piece to the batting and backing.
4. Stitch along the drawn line. Using pinking shears, cut ⅛" to ¼" outside the stitched line. Your completed foundation should look like the illustration below.

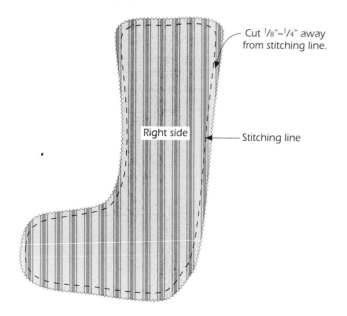

Cut ⅛"–¼" away from stitching line.

Right side

Stitching line

Wreath

1. Layer the batting on the backing fabric. Smooth the batting and backing, working out from the center.
2. Make a plastic template for the wreath. Trace the template on the right side of the 14" x 18" green wreath background. Do not cut yet.
3. Pin this piece to the batting and backing.
4. Stitch along the drawn lines. Using pinking shears, cut ⅛" to ¼" outside the stitched lines. Your completed foundation should look like the illustration below.

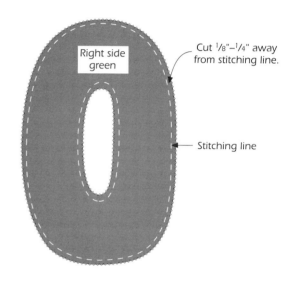

Right side green

Cut ⅛"–¼" away from stitching line.

Stitching line

Reindeer

1. Layer the batting on the backing fabric. Smooth the batting and backing, working out from the center.
2. Make plastic templates for the reindeer's head and antlers. Trace the templates onto the right side of the fabrics described in the "Materials" list. Do not cut yet.

3. Pin the 8" x 10" brown background to the batting and backing. Align the 8" edge with the bottom edge of the batting, 3" from the left edge.

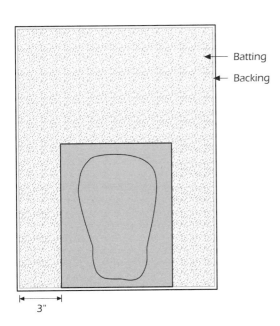

5. Stitch around the reindeer head and antlers along the drawn lines. Using pinking shears, cut ⅛" to ¼" outside the stitched lines. Your completed foundation should look like the illustration below.

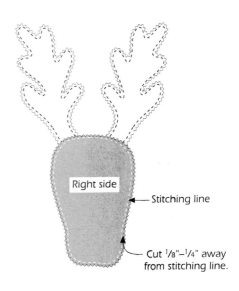

4. Pin the two 5" x 10" muslin antler backgrounds under the top of the 8" x 10" brown background as shown below. Line up the lower edges of the antlers with the top of the drawn reindeer head. Position the antlers so the curve of the design is toward the center.

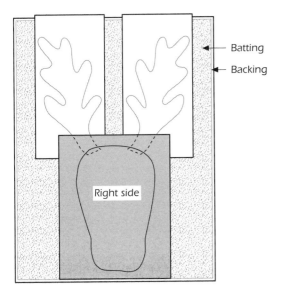

Appliquilt

Use the templates on pages 61–63 and on the pullout pattern. Refer to the templates and the quilt plan on page 57 for layout. The numbers on the templates indicate the stitching order.

Stocking

1. Make plastic templates for the heel, toe, cuff, and tree.
2. Cut the appliqué pieces from the fabrics described in the "Materials" list.
3. Sew the pieces in place, stitching through all the layers (see the photo on page 24 for placement).

Wreath

1. Make a plastic template for the yo-yos.
2. Cut 50 circles from the fabrics described in the "Materials" list.
3. Make the yo-yos, following the directions on page 15. I used 60 yo-yos, but you may not want to overlap them as much as I did. You can always make more.
4. Stitch the yo-yos to the wreath with buttons and an occasional red wooden bead.

Reindeer

1. Make plastic templates for the reindeer's blaze and halter.
2. Cut the appliqué pieces from the fabrics described in the "Materials" list.
3. Sew the blaze and halter pieces in place, stitching through all the layers.

Embellishments

Refer to the templates and the quilt plan on page 57 for placement.

Stocking

1. Sew on buttons.
2. Tie 12"-long pieces of jute to the stars.
3. Tie the pieces of jute in a bow and stitch the bow to the stocking cuff.

Wreath

To make the ribbon, cut 1 strip, 3" x 36", from the red plaid. Tie the strip into a bow and adjust the ends. Stitch the bow to the bottom of the wreath.

Reindeer

1. Trace the leaf onto the right side of 2 pieces of green fabric, each 2" x 3". Cut 1 piece, 2" x 3", of batting and place it between the leaf pieces.
2. Stitch along the drawn line. Using pinking shears, cut 1/8" to 1/4" outside the stitched line.
3. Position the leaf and sew buttons in one corner to attach.
4. Sew on buttons for eyes, nose, and halter strap.

There are all sorts of neat ways to hang these quilts! For example, you can paint clothespins and use the pins to hang the quilts from a string of jute. Or attach drapery rings or cloth tabs to the quilt backs. Be creative.

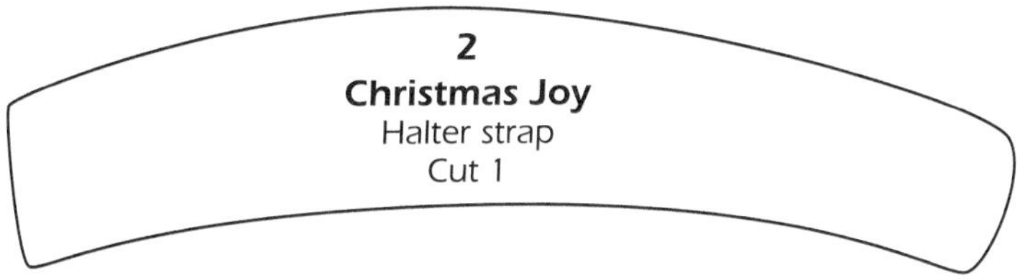

2
Christmas Joy
Halter strap
Cut 1

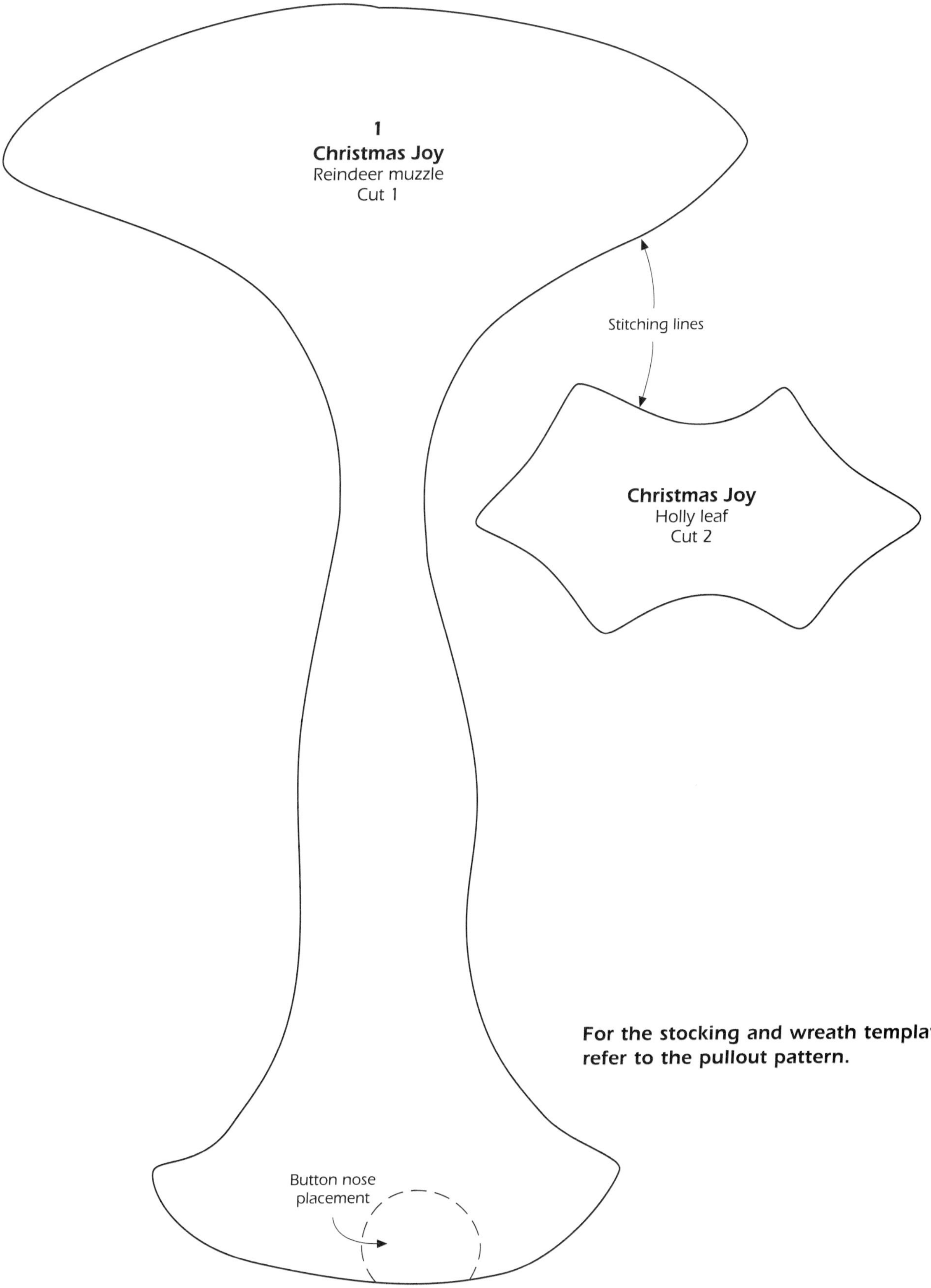

1
Christmas Joy
Reindeer muzzle
Cut 1

Stitching lines

Christmas Joy
Holly leaf
Cut 2

For the stocking and wreath templates,
refer to the pullout pattern.

Button nose
placement

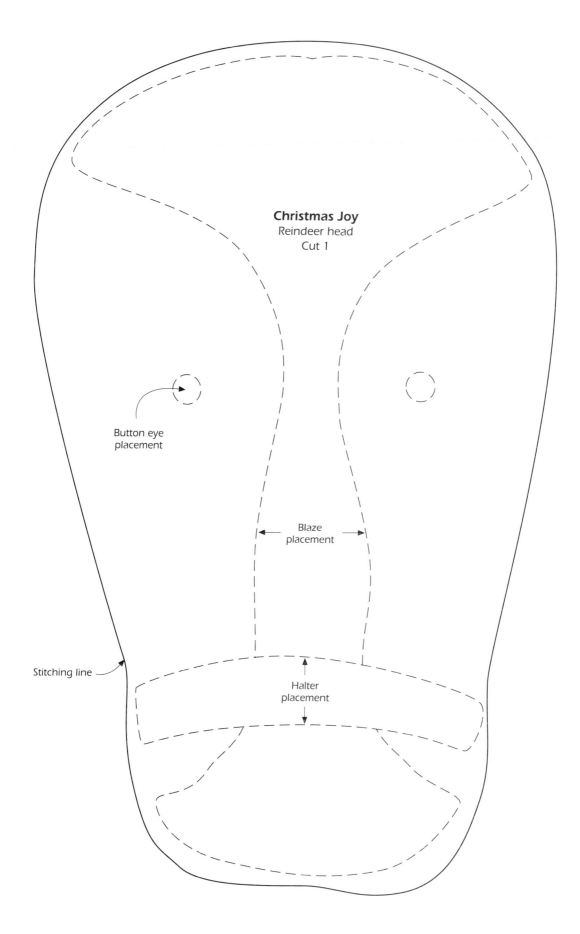

Christmas Joy
Reindeer head
Cut 1

Button eye
placement

Blaze
placement

Stitching line

Halter
placement

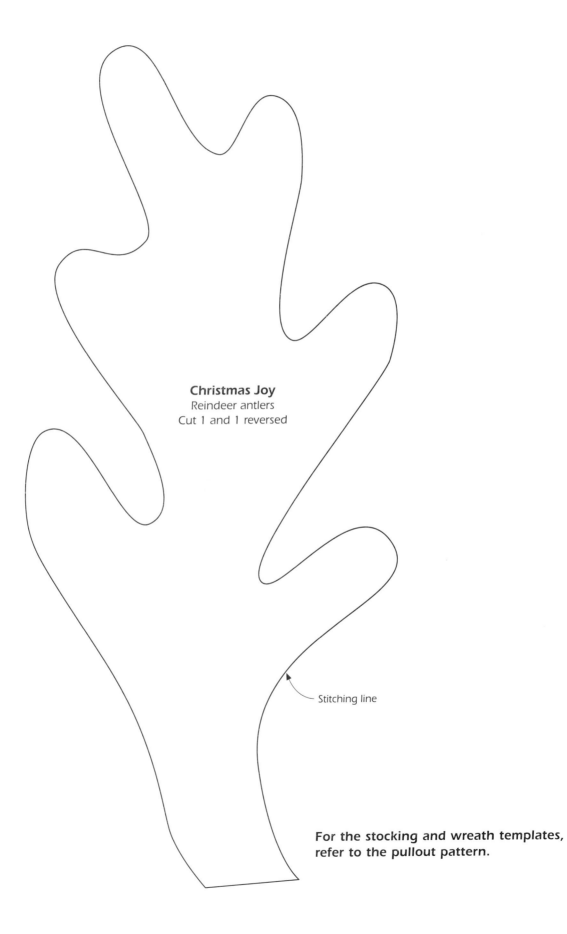

Christmas Joy
Reindeer antlers
Cut 1 and 1 reversed

Stitching line

For the stocking and wreath templates, refer to the pullout pattern.

'Tis the Season

Here's a great quilt that uses all the techniques covered in this book. It has all the ingredients for a really fun holiday.

Color Photo: page 19
Size: 46" x 40"
Materials: 44"-wide fabric

1 ½ yds. beige plaid for background

¾ yd. green plaid for border and lattice (sashing between the blocks)*

⅓ yd. red-and-green plaid for Santa

¼ yd. brown for sleigh

¼ yd. red stripe for binding

1 ½ yds. of 45"-wide fabric or 2 yds. of 44"-wide fabric for backing (You need to piece the backing if you use 44"-wide fabric.)

1 ½ yds. Pellon fleece or other thin batting

Scraps:

   ¼ yd. Warm & Natural batting for snowman, Santa's beard, and Santa's suit trim

   ½ yd. total of 6 greens for tree in sleigh, holly leaves, yo-yo wreath, button trees, and Santa's pocket

⅜ yd. total of plaids for ribbon, snowman scarf, angel dress, package, letters, and patch on bag

Grunged muslin (see page 7) for angel's wings and North Pole sign

Yellow for halo

Muslin for angel's face

Burlap for Santa's bag

Brown for sign post

Gold embroidery floss for watch chain

#8 perle cotton in assorted colors

1 yd. each of green and plain jute

Assorted buttons for sleigh, tree, borders, sign, Santa, small trees, and halo

3 cinnamon star buttons for Star block

Gingerbread man button for Santa's bag

Embellishments of your choice, such as red beads, bells, plastic Christmas lights, Santa's list, toys, reindeer feed bag, and Santa's pocket watch

Miniature quilt, approximately 5½" square

*If you want to use different fabrics for the border and lattice, you need ⅜ yard for each.

Making the Foundation
Cutting

'Tis the Season Cutting Plan
The measurements shown include ¼"-wide seam allowances.

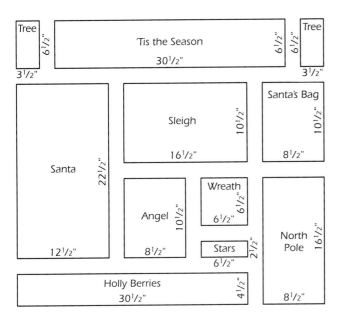

From the beige plaid fabric, cut:
the backgrounds for each block, referring to the cutting plan for measurements.

From the green plaid fabric, cut:
2 strips, each 3½" x 40½", for side borders
2 strips, each 2½" x 40½", for top and bottom borders
1 strip, 2½" x 8½", for lattice
1 strip, 2½" x 28½", for lattice
3 strips, each 2½" x 6½", for lattice
1 strip, 2½" x 10½", for lattice
1 strip, 2½" x 16½", for lattice
1 strip, 2½" x 22½", for lattice
1 strip, 2½" x 30½", for lattice
1 strip, 2½" x 40½", for lattice

I used the same fabric for both the borders and the lattice strips on my quilt. If you want to try this approach, I recommend that you wait until after you have pieced your foundation to cut the borders.

Unit Construction
All seams are ¼" wide.

Refer to the 'Tis the Season Construction Plan below. Construct the units in order, beginning with Unit 1.

'Tis the Season Construction Plan

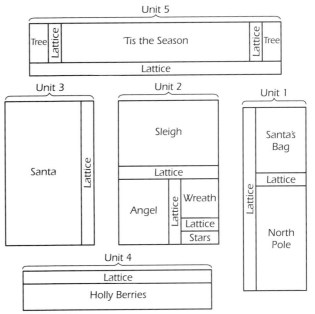

Unit 1

When finished, this unit should measure 10½" x 28½".

1. With right sides together, sew the Santa's Bag block background and the North Pole block background together with the 2½" x 8½" lattice strip between them. Press the seams.
2. Sew the 2½" x 28½" lattice strip, right sides together, on the left edge. Press the seam.

Unit 2

When finished, this unit should measure 16½" x 22½".

1. With right sides together, sew the Wreath block background and the Stars block background together with a 2½" x 6½" lattice strip between them. Press the seams. This unit should measure 6½" x 10½".
2. Sew the Angel block background and the 6½" x 10½" unit constructed in step 1 together with the 2½" x 10½" lattice strip between them. Press the seams. This unit should measure 10½" x 16½".
3. With right sides together, sew the Sleigh block background to the top of the 10½" x 16½" unit, with the 2½" x 16½" lattice strip between them. Press the seams.

Unit 3

When finished, this unit should measure 14½" x 22½".

With right sides together, sew the 2½" x 22½" lattice strip to the right edge of the Santa block background. Press the seam.

Unit 4

When finished, this unit should measure 6½" x 30½".

With right sides together, sew the 2½" x 30½" lattice strip to the top edge of the Holly Berries block background. Press the seam.

Unit 5

When finished, this unit should measure 6½" x 40½".

1. With right sides together, sew the Tree block backgrounds and the 'Tis the Season block background together with 2½" x 6½" lattice strips between them. Press the seams.
2. With right sides together, sew the 2½" x 40½" lattice strip to the bottom edge of the unit constructed in step 1. Press the seam.

Assembly

1. Sew the left edge of Unit 2 to the right edge of Unit 3. Press the seam. Next, sew the top edge of Unit 4 to the bottom edge of the unit constructed from Units 2 and 3. Press the seam. The finished unit should measure 28½" x 30½".
2. Sew Unit 1 to the unit constructed in step 1. Press the seam. The finished unit should measure 28½" x 40½".
3. Sew Unit 5 to the unit constructed in step 2. Press the seam. The pieced top should measure 36½" x 40½". Because of differences in your seam allowances (even very slight ones) and the stretchiness of your fabrics, the size of the top may not be exactly the size specified when finished. If you have been consistent with your seam allowance, the blocks and units should fit together nicely. You're not wrong, just different.
4. Measure the outer edges of the quilt top carefully. Opposite sides should, but may not, measure the same. If the quilt top's opposing side measurements differ, either take an average of the two sides or measure through the middle of the quilt top and use that measurement to cut the borders. The border strips you sew on opposing sides should be the same measurement so the quilt will hang straight. With right sides together, sew the side borders to the pieced top. Press the seams. Repeat this procedure for the top and bottom borders.
5. Depending on the width of your fabric, you may need to piece the backing. Layer the batting on the backing fabric. Smooth the batting and backing, working out from the center. See "Making the Quilt Sandwich Foundation" on page 10.
6. Machine or hand quilt in-the-ditch around the blocks.
7. Bind the edges with 1½"-wide strips of fabric, following the directions on page 13.

Appliquilt

Use the templates on pages 68–71 and the pullout pattern. Refer to the templates and the quilt plan on page 64 for layout. The numbers on the templates indicate the stitching order. Read the following instructions carefully before you begin stitching. Instructions are given block by block.

1. Make plastic templates following the directions on page 11.
2. Cut the appliqué pieces from the fabrics described in the "Materials" list.
3. **Santa block.** For Santa's pocket, fold the top of the square over about ½" on the right side of the fabric and stitch in place. To give Santa's beard texture, stitch broken lines (shown on the template).

4. **Sleigh block.** Place the edge of a miniature quilt under the top of the sleigh before stitching. I purchased this small quilt, but you could make your own.

5. **Santa's Bag block.** Stitch patch to bag before stitching bag to quilt. Cut a 40"-long piece of thread. Start stitching in the upper left corner of the bag, leaving a 10"-long tail. Stitch through all the layers around the left, bottom, and right sides. On the top edge of the bag, stitch through the burlap only. Do not stitch the top of the bag to the quilt. End your stitching on the top of the quilt and tie a knot. Trim the thread if necessary and tie a bell to each end.

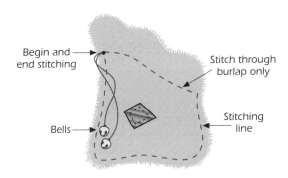

Begin and end stitching

Stitch through burlap only

Bells

Stitching line

6. **North Pole block.** Stitch the snowman and signpost in place. Using a transfer pen, trace "North Pole" onto the grunged muslin for the North Pole Sign. Embroider the lettering.

7. **Wreath block.** Make 8 yo-yos, following the directions on page 15.

8. **Angel block.** Stitch the angel in place, following the sequence marked on the templates.

9. **Holly Berries block.** Stitch the leaves in place.

10. **Button Tree blocks.** Using pinking shears or the pinking blade of a rotary cutter, cut the following strips from the 6 green fabrics:

> 2 strips, each $\frac{1}{2}$" x 5$\frac{1}{2}$", for tree trunks
> 2 strips each of the following for branches:
> $\frac{1}{2}$" x 1$\frac{1}{2}$"
> $\frac{1}{2}$" x 2"
> $\frac{1}{2}$" x 2$\frac{1}{2}$"
> $\frac{1}{2}$" x 3"

Sew buttons to the branch strips to hold them in place. Stitch through the bottom of the tree trunk, leaving a knot on top of the quilt.

11. **'Tis the Season block.** Stitch the lettering in place.

Embellishments

1. **Santa block.** Using embroidery floss, make a braid approximately 6" long. Attach one end to the top of the pocket and the other end behind the watch button. Sew on a large button, the watch button, and small buttons or beads for eyes.

2. **Sleigh block.** Sew buttons to the sleigh and tree as shown in the quilt photo. Attach reindeer feed bag.

3. **Santa's Bag block.** Tuck Santa's list inside the bag and stitch in place. Fold a piece of quilt batting and wrap a scrap of fabric around it, stitching fabric folds in place with thread. The package is approximately 3" x 5". Tie the fabric package with jute. Stitch or glue the cinnamon gingerbread man to the package. Tuck the package in Santa's bag and stitch in place.

4. **Angel block.** Sew buttons on the angel's halo and dress.

5. **Wreath block.** Cut a 1$\frac{1}{2}$" x 18$\frac{1}{2}$" strip from the fabric in the "Materials" list and tie a bow. Stitch to the top of the wreath. Adjust the bow and trim the ends, if desired.

6. **Star block.** Sew 3 cinnamon star buttons on the background block.

7. **North Pole block.** Tie 7 plastic Christmas lights to a 16" piece of jute. Starting 4" from the end, place a light approximately every 2". Stitch the ends of the jute to the top and bottom of the pole. Sew buttons on the sign and snowmen.

8. **Holly Berries block.** Lay green jute along the bases of the leaves. Attach it to the quilt by sewing clusters of red beads over the jute.

9. Sew buttons on the borders and lattices.

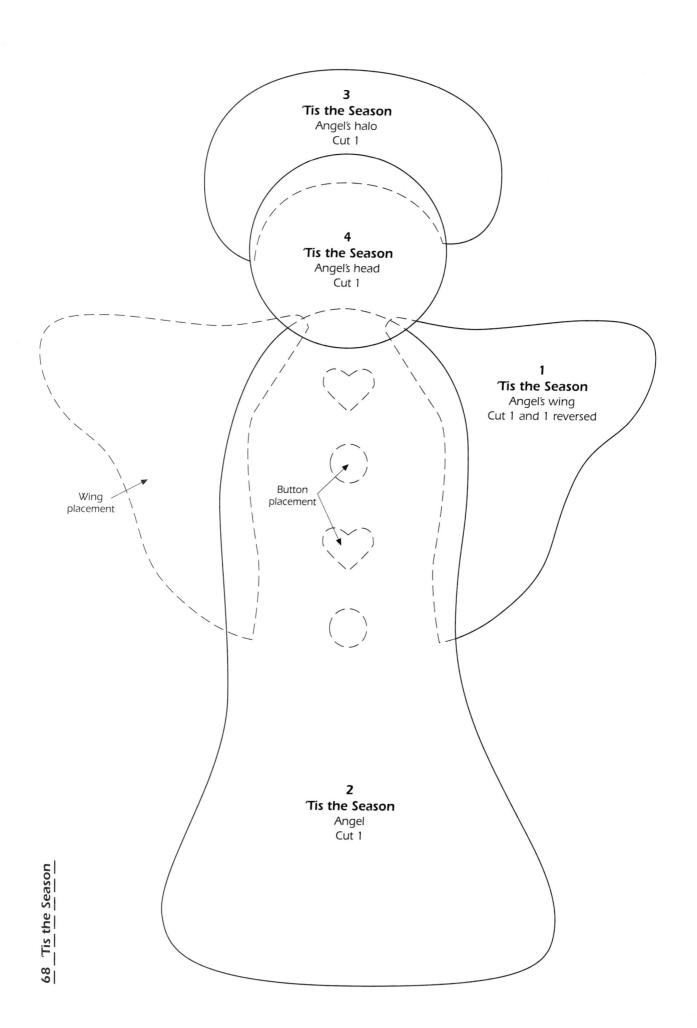

3
'Tis the Season
Angel's halo
Cut 1

4
'Tis the Season
Angel's head
Cut 1

1
'Tis the Season
Angel's wing
Cut 1 and 1 reversed

Wing
placement

Button
placement

2
'Tis the Season
Angel
Cut 1

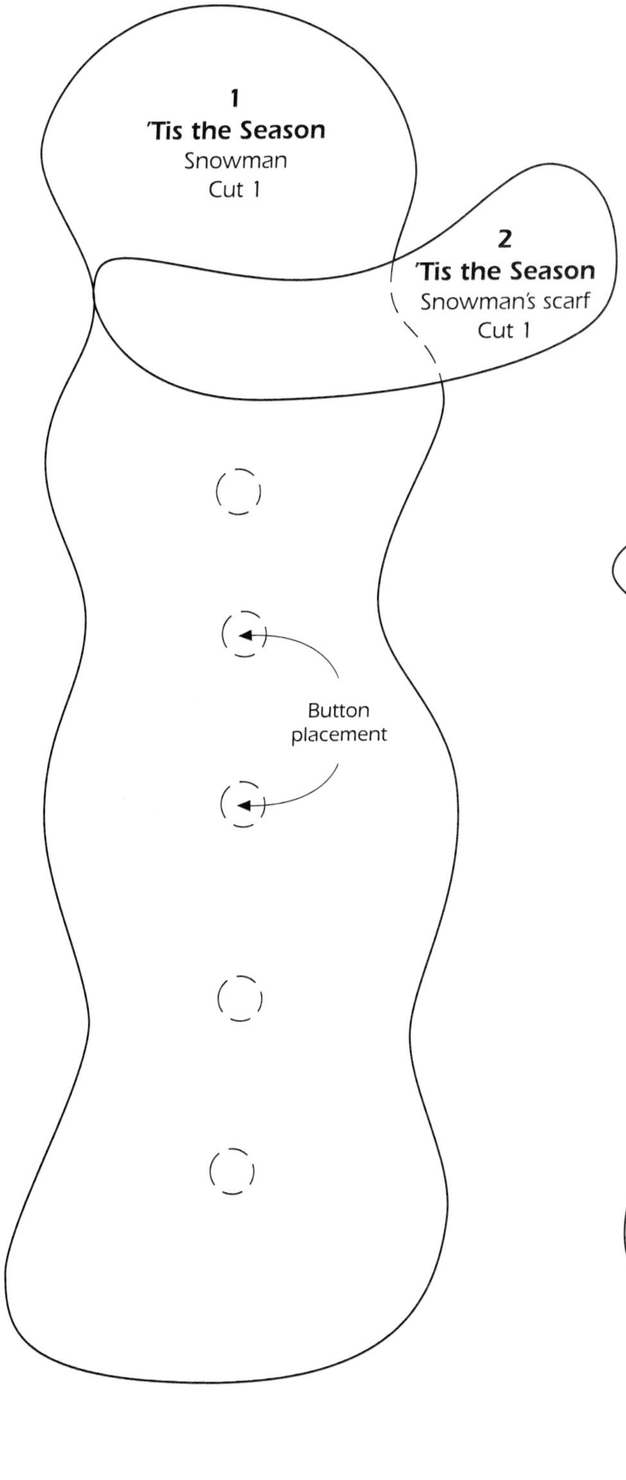

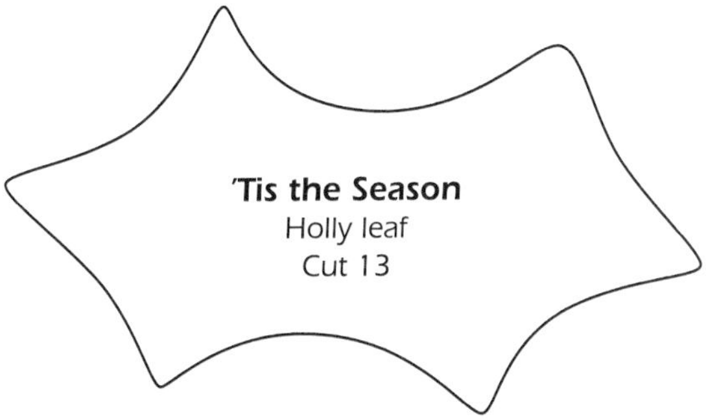

1
'Tis the Season
Snowman
Cut 1

2
'Tis the Season
Snowman's scarf
Cut 1

'Tis the Season
Holly leaf
Cut 13

2
'Tis the Season
Signpost
Cut 1

Button placement

Button
placement

NORTH
POLE

'Tis the Season
Sign
Cut 1

For the Santa and signpost templates,
refer to the pullout pattern.

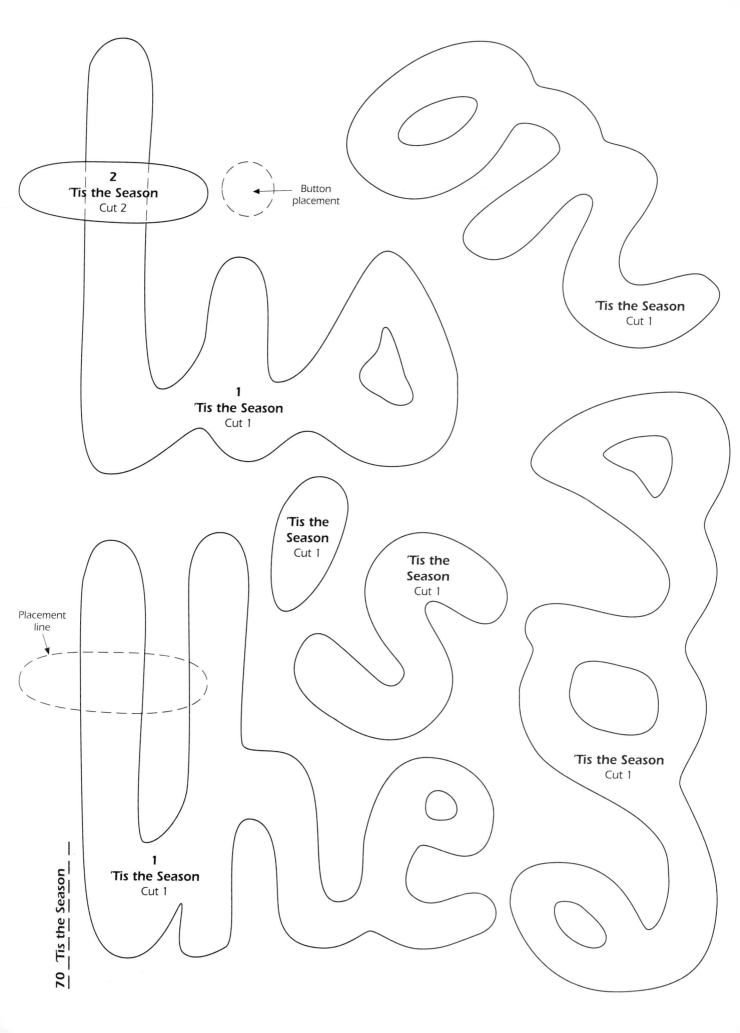

2
'Tis the Season
Cut 2

Button
placement

'Tis the Season
Cut 1

1
'Tis the Season
Cut 1

'Tis the
Season
Cut 1

'Tis the
Season
Cut 1

'Tis the Season
Cut 1

Placement
line

1
'Tis the Season
Cut 1

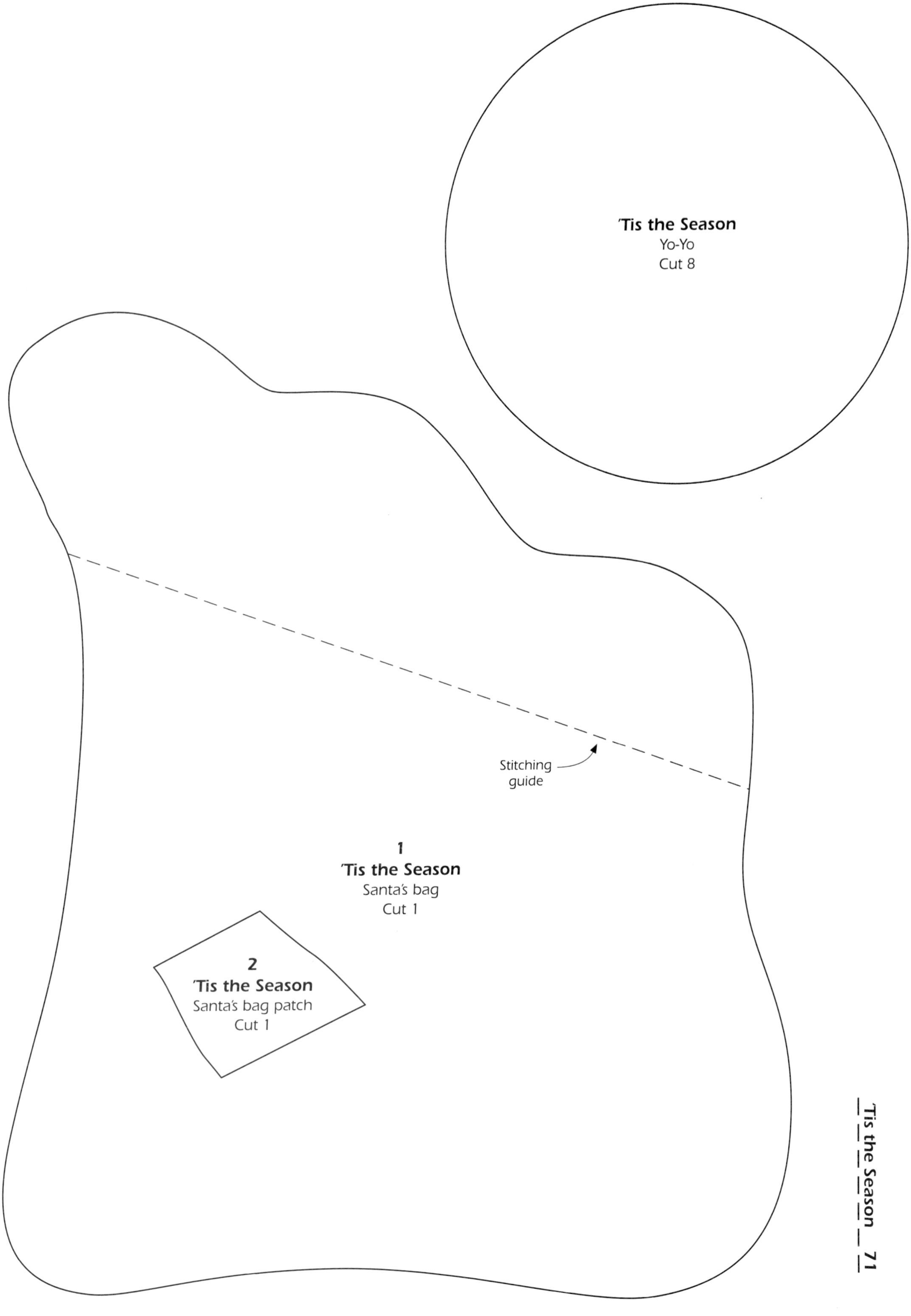

'Tis the Season
Yo-Yo
Cut 8

Stitching
guide

1
'Tis the Season
Santa's bag
Cut 1

2
'Tis the Season
Santa's bag patch
Cut 1

That Patchwork Place Publications and Products

4", 6", 8", & metric Bias Square® • BiRangle™ • Ruby Beholder™ • Pineapple Rule • ScrapMaster • Rotary Rule™ • Rotary Mate™
Shortcuts to America's Best-Loved Quilts (video)

Many titles are available at your local quilt shop. For more information, send $2 for a color catalog to
That Patchwork Place, Inc., PO Box 118, Bothell WA 98041-0118 USA.

☎ Call 1-800-426-3126 for the name and location of the quilt shop nearest you.